INSTANT

FRENCH

by Dorothy Thomas

Language adviser
Jean-Marc Capello

Illustrated by

apropos design

dot publications

The *Instant* series developed out of the author's experiences teaching adults, as a response to their need to say things quickly, even – or especially – about matters which they had not yet studied. Dorothy Thomas was a student at the Universities of Newcastle upon Tyne and Oslo and is an associate of the Institute of Translation and Interpreting. When not travelling the world talking to people, her main interest is music.

to the memory of
David Thomas
without whom dot Publications
would not exist

Published by dot Publications, 54a Haig Avenue, Whitley Bay NE25 8JD

First published 1988 Third edition 2000
Copyright © D M Thomas 2000

ISBN 1 871086 09 4

The author would particularly like to thank Louis Perry, Jacqueline Gleize-Bourras, Roberta Carruthers, Stephen Govier and Roger Booth for their patience and assistance.

la *France* – France
la *Belgique* – Belgium   la *Suisse* – Switzerland

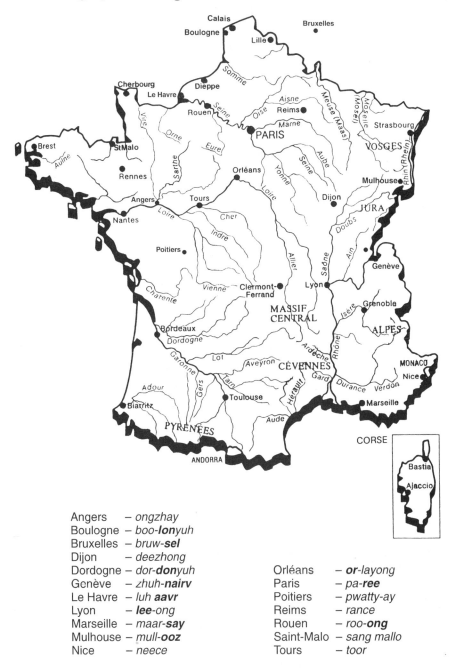

Angers	– *ongzhay*		
Boulogne	– *boo-**lonyuh***		
Bruxelles	– *bruw-**sel***		
Dijon	– *deezhong*		
Dordogne	– *dor-**donyuh***	Orléans	– ***or**-layong*
Genève	– *zhuh-**nairv***	Paris	– *pa-**ree***
Le Havre	– *luh **aavr***	Poitiers	– *pwatty-ay*
Lyon	– ***lee**-ong*	Reims	– *rance*
Marseille	– *maar-**say***	Rouen	– *roo-**ong***
Mulhouse	– *mull-**ooz***	Saint-Malo	– *sang mallo*
Nice	– *neece*	Tours	– *toor*

◼4 *Contents*

Using this book

Even if you have never learned another language, this book will help you get by, so that you can get what you need or wherever you want to go.

Right at the back is a list of **basic phrases** covering such essentials as *yes, no, who, what, where, I don't understand* – and *Help!*

Opposite this are **numbers**, from 0 to a million. It's worth learning some of these – numbers are a vital part of any language and make it much easier to buy things or make arrangements. Incidentally, **time** is on p. 53, next to the **alphabet**.

If you want a particular item, first look it up in the **Contents** or the **Dictionary/ Index** (French p. 96, English p. 100). We then take you through a series of typical situations, giving the words you need followed by an idea of the replies you are likely to hear. Follow the speech guide under each picture. The guide to **sounds** on p. 6 will help you pronounce things correctly.

Most situations follow a basic pattern which you can use in other places. For example, most of the phrases for the baker's on p. 37 can be used in other shops too. Sentences have been designed to be interchangeable, so if you want something different from what is in the picture, just slot it in.

Brackets: words in brackets are alternatives, eg (sir/madam).

Food: there is a comprehensive guide to French menu terms on pp. 30-35, with a few English ones at the end. Both English and French names are given for **meat** p. 38, **fish** p. 39, **fruit** and **vegetables** pp. 40-41 and **groceries** p. 42.

If you want to find out more about how the language works, on pp. 94-95 is a short section which will give you an insight into French **grammar**.

Unlike English, which has different greetings for morning and afternoon, *bonjour* is used all day in French. Since it is a more formal language than English, it is customary to add *monsieur* or *madame*, so that when talking to someone you will say *bonjour, monsieur* or *madame* (though we have sometimes had to omit this for reasons of space). A good way of attracting someone's attention is to say, *s'il vous plaît, monsieur* (or *madame*).

Remember, travel should be fun. If you can talk to people and understand some of the things you see about you, you will enjoy it much more. Don't be shy, have a go! Even if you don't get it absolutely perfect, the fact that you've tried will be much appreciated.

Enjoy yourself, have a good trip, and – ***Bon voyage!***

It is impossible to convey the sounds of one language in those of another, but the transcription given here will enable you to produce a rough approximation.

Stress In English words one syllable is stressed heavily, but in French all syllables have equal stress and the emphasis tends to fall on the last syllable of each sentence or group of words (this has been shown by putting the stressed letters in **heavy** type). Some words are split by a **hyphen** to make them easier to read and to get the stress in the right place. Pronounce them as one word, with no gaps.

Nasal vowels (ain, am, em, en, im, in, on, un): these resemble **ng** in sing or long, but don't stress the **g**, it should barely be heard (shown as *ong, ang,* etc).

a, à, â a wide sound between the **a** in mat and in father.
ais, ait, aient all sound like **eh**, or **a** in late, ie with no consonant at the end. So do **é, er, ez**.
au, eau are pronounced **oh**.
è, ê like **e** in met, but **e** can also resemble **a** in Emma.
i like **ee** in meet.
eu like **ur** in fur, but without pronouncing the **r**.
   (exception: **eu** from avoir is pronounced like French **u**).
o like **o** in hot, but **oh** at the end of words.
oi like **wa** in wagon; exception: oignon *(onyong)*.
ou as **ou** in you.
u easy for Scots, hard for everyone else. Purse your lips as if about to whistle, then say it as it looks.
ui like **wee** in week.

ci is always pronounced **see**: spécial *(spayss-yal)*.
ch like **sh** in she.
ç like **s** in see.
g before a, o, u as in go; before e, i, y like **s** in measure.
gn like **ni** in onion.
h always silent.
j like **s** in measure.
qu like **k** in key.
r erupts from the back of the throat. Try gargling.
s usually as in sit, but silent at the end of a word*.
t as in too, but **s** in -tion: station*(stassyong)*.
th like **t** in too.

*****Liaison** Consonants are often silent at the end of a word, but if the next one begins with a vowel, **s** and **x** (both pronounced z in this context) and **n** are usually joined onto it, eg les enfants *(lay zonfon)*..

Capital letters French uses these for proper names and places, but not for days of the week. We have used them sometimes to make it easier to pick out words on a page.

Booking accommodation

Madame/Monsieur,   Dear Sir or Madam,

Hotels
Je voudrais réserver   *une chambre simple*   *(deux chambres simples)*
I would like to book   one single room   (two single rooms)

une chambre double   *(deux chambres doubles)*   *une chambre familiale*
one double room   (two double rooms)   a family room

avec salle de bain/douche   *pour – nuit(s) du – au – .*
with bath/shower   for – night(s) from – to – .

Camping
*Je voudrais réserver un emplacement (à l'ombre/avec branchement électrique)
dans votre terrain de camping. Je souhaiterais rester – nuit (nuits) du – au – .*

I would like to book a pitch (in the shade/with electricity) on your campsite. I wish
to stay – night (nights) from – to – .

Nous possédons   une voiture/une caravane/un camping-car
We have   a car/a caravan/a motor caravan

et une grande/petite tente (avec auvent).
and a large/small tent (with awning).

* * *

Est-ce que vous avez des installations pour personnes handicapées?
Have you any facilities for the disabled?

Je me sers d'un fauteuil roulant.   *J'ai besoin d'une chambre au rez-de-chaussée.*
I use a wheelchair.   I need a room on the ground floor.

* * *

Nous serons – adulte(s) et – enfant(s) âgé (âgés)* de – an (ans)*.
We shall be – adult(s) and – child(ren) aged – .   *if more than one

Veuillez me communiquer vos tarifs.
Please let me know your rates.

*A combien s'élèvent les arrhes pour la réservation de la chambre (des chambres)/
de l'emplacement?*
How much deposit do you require to book the room (the rooms)/the pitch?

Je vous prie d'agrécr l'expression de mes salutations distinguées,
Yours faithfully,

8 Hotels

French hotel prices are quoted per room, not per person, with breakfast usually an optional extra. It's quite normal to inspect the room, so if you would like one that is bigger, smaller or quieter, just say so. Prefer something less exotic? – **chambre d'hôte** means 'bed and breakfast'.

If you've booked

2. Bonjour, madame.

3. Mon nom est – . J'ai réservé une chambre pour ce soir.

1. Bonjour, monsieur.

4. Ah oui, c'est la chambre numero dix.

5. Votre passeport, s'il vous plaît. Voulez-vous signer ici?

1. *Bong-zhoor, mus-**yuh**.*
   Good morning/afternoon, sir.

2. *Bong-zhoor, ma-**dam**.*
   Good morning/afternoon, madam.

3. *Mong nom ay – . Zhay rayzairvay uwn shombr poor suh **swaar**.*
   My name is – . I've booked a room for tonight.

4. *Ah wee, sayla shombr **nuw**mayro deece.*
   Oh yes, it's room 10.

5. *Votr passpor, seelvoo-**play**. **Vool**ayvoo seenyay ee-**see**?*
   Could I have your passport, please? Please sign here.

---

1. Où peut-on se garer?

2. Quel est votre numéro d'immatriculation?

1. *Oo purtong suh garray?*
   Where can I/we park?

2. *Kellay votr **nuw**mayro deema-treekoo-**lass**yong?*
   What's your registration number?

P

une nuit
uwn nwee
one night

deux nuits
dur nwee
two nights

une semaine
uwn suh-men
a/one week

1. Bonsoir, monsieur. Vous avez une chambre de libre?

If you haven't booked

2. Oui. Pour combien de personnes?

3. Pour une personne (deux personnes), et un enfant (deux enfants).

4. Bien. C'est pour combien de nuits, monsieur?

5. Pour (deux nuits/une semaine).

. *Bong-swaar, mus-yuh. Voo-zavvay uwn shombr duh leebr?*
    Good evening, sir. Have you a room available?

. *Wee. Poor komb-yang duh pair-sonn?*
    Certainly, how many for?

. *Poor uwn pair-sonn (dur...), ay uhn onfonn (dur zonfonn).*
    For one (two...) person/s, and one child (two children).

. *Byang. Say poor komb-yang duh nwee, mus-yuh?*
    Fine. How long for, sir?

. *Poor (dur nwee/uwn suh-men).*
    For (two nights/a week).

Désolé, c'est complet
Dayzollay, say komplay.
Sorry, we're full.

Il y a un autre hôtel près d'ici?
Eel-ya uwn ohtro-tell pray dee-see?
Is there another hotel nearby?

In towns the Tourist Office will help you find a room (most speak English). Look for **Syndicat d'Initiative** or **Office de Tourisme**. (N.B. *Hôtel de Ville* is the town hall and *Hôtel-Dieu* the hospital.)

2. Une chambre double
(et une chambre familiale).

4. Avec douche et toilettes.

5. Vous avez un lit d'enfant?

1. Est-ce que vous désirez une chambre double ou pour une personne?

3. Avec bain, douche, toilettes?

1. *Esskuh voo day-**zee**ray uwn shombr doobl oo poor uwn pair-**sonn**?*
   Would you like a double room or a single?

2. *Uwn shombr doobl (ay uwn shombr fameel-**yal**).*
   A double room (and a family room).

3. *Avvek bang, doosh, twa-**let**?*
   With bath, shower, toilet?

4. *Avvek doosh ay twa-**let**.*
   With shower and toilet.

5. *Voo-**zavv**ay uhn **lee don**fonn?*
   Could I have a child's bed, please?

pour une personne
*poor uwn pair-**sonn***
a single bed

un grand lit
uhn gron lee
a double bed

des lits jumeaux
day lee zhuwmo
twin beds

la douche
la doosh
the shower

le bain
luh bang
the bath

les toilettes
*lay twa-**let***
the lavatory

Talking to staff: pp.14, 15

2. Bien. C'est combien?

4. Très bien. Je la prends.

6. Voilà. Je m'appelle – .

1. Oui, on a encore une chambre.

3. C'est – francs la nuit.

5. Bien. Votre nom, s'il vous plaît, et votre passeport.

7. Voulez-vous signer ici?

8. Merci. Voici la clé de votre chambre.

1. *Wee, onna ong-kor uwn **shombr**.*
   Yes, we have a room.

2. *Byang. Say komb-yang?*
   Good. How much is it?

3. *Say – frong la **nwee**.*
   It's – francs a night.

4. *Tray byang. Zhulla **pron**.*
   Fine. I'll take it.

5. *Byang. Votr nom, seelvoo-**play**, ay votr passpor.*
   Good. Your name, please, and your passport.

6. *Vwa-**la**. Zhumma-**pell** – .*
   Here you are. My name is – .

7. ***Vool**ayvoo seenyay ee-**see**?*
   Could you sign here?

8. *Mair-**see**. Vwa-**see** la klay duh votr shombr.*
   Thank you. Here's the key to your room.

La clé, s'il vous plaît. Chambre numéro dix-huit.
*La klay, seelvoo-**play**. Shombr **nuw**mayro deez-**weet**.*
Could I have my key, please? It's room 18.

1. Pourrais-je voir la chambre?
2. Oui, bien sûr.
3. C'est bien. Je la prends.
6. Non, je regrette, monsieur...
4. Non, elle est trop bruyante (chère).
5. En auriez-vous une (plus tranquille/moins chère)?

1. *Pooray zhuh vwaar la* **shombr**?
   Can I see the room?

2. *Wee, byang* **suwr**.
   Yes, of course.

3. *Say byang. Zhulla* **pron**.
   That's fine. I'll take it.

4. *Nong, ellay troh brweeyont (shair).*
   No, it's too noisy (expensive).

5. *On* **oh**ree-ay voo uwn (pluw trong-**kee**/mwang shair)?
   Have you a (quieter/cheaper) one?

6. *Nong, zhuh rug-**ret**, mus-**yuh**...*
   'No. I'm sorry, sir...'

au premier/second étage
*oh prumyay/suh-**gawn** ay-**tazh***
on the first/second floor

au rez-de-chaussée (RC)
*oh rayda **shohsay***
on the ground floor (US 1st)

l'ascenseur
*lasson-**sur***
the lift

1. Je voudrais une chambre au rez-de-chaussée.

2. Est-ce qu'il y a un ascenseur?

1. *Zhuh voodray uwn shombro rayda **shoh**sa*
   I'd like a room on the ground floor.

2. *Eskeel-**ya** uhn asson-**sur**?*
   Is there a lift?

1. Le petit déjeuner est-il compris?

4. A quelle heure servez-vous (le petit déjeuner/le déjeuner/le dîner)?

2. Le petit déjeuner est (en supplément/compris).

3. A quelle heure voulez-vous prendre votre petit déjeuner?

5. De 7.30 à 10.

1. Pourrais-je avoir ma note, s'il vous plaît?

1. *Luh putty **day**zhurnay etteel kom-**pree**?*
   Is breakfast included?

2. *Luh putty **day**zhurnay ett (on **sup**laymong/kom-**pree**).*
   Breakfast is (extra/included).

3. *A kell-**ur vool**ayvoo prondr votr putty **day**zhurnay?*
   What time would you like breakfast?

4. *A kell-**ur** sairvay-voo luh (putty **day**zhurnay/**day**zhurnay/**dee**nay)?*
   What time do you serve (breakfast/lunch/dinner)?

5. *Duh settur tront a **deece**.*
   From 7.30 to 10.*

*Time p.53

*Time p.53

Checking out

1. Pourrais-je avoir ma note, s'il vous plaît?

2. Je voudrais payer (en travellers/avec ma carte bancaire).

3. Pourrais-je avoir un reçu, s'il vous plaît?

4. Merci pour tout. Au revoir, (monsieur/madame).

. *Pooray zhav-**waar** ma not, seelvoo-**play**?*
   Could I have the bill, please?

. *Zhuh voodray payay (on trav-**lair**/avvek ma kaart bong-**kair**).*
   I'd like to pay (by traveller's cheque/by credit card).

. *Pooray zhav-**waar** uhn rus-**suw**, seelvoo-**play**?*
   Could I have a receipt, please?

. *Mair-**see** poor **too**. Oh ruv-**waar**, (mus-**yuh**/ma-**dam**).*
   Thanks for everything. Goodbye, (sir/madam).

| Taxe de séjour = Tourist tax |
| Toutes taxes comprises/TTC = All taxes included |

la CHEMINÉE	la PORTE	l'ÉGOUT	le TUYAU d'ÉVACUATION	la CLÔTURE
la shummy-nay	*la port*	*lay-**goo***	*twee-yo dayvakkuw-**as**yong*	*la kloh-**tuwr***
the Chimney	the Door	the Drain	the Drainpipe	the Fence

le JARDIN
luh zhardang
the Garden

les CLÉS
lay klay
the Keys

une ÉCHELLE
*uwn ay-**shell***
a Ladder

la SERRURE
*la ser-**ruwr***
the Lock

le TOIT
luh twa
the Roof

la FOSSE
SEPTIQUE
*la foss sep-**teek***
the Septic Tank

une TUILE
uwn tweel
a Tile

le MUR
luh muwr
the Wall

General matters

1. Excusez-moi, je cherche (Monsieur/ Madame) – .
   *Exkuwzay-**mwa**, zhuh shairsh (mus-**yuh**/ ma-**dam**) – .*
   Excuse me, I'm looking for (Mr/ Mrs) – .

2. Où habite- (t-il/ t-elle)?
   *Oo a-**beet** (teel/ tell)?*
   Where does (he/ she) live?

3. Il nous faut (des tasses/ encore des tasses).
   *Eel noo foh (day tass/ ong-**kor** day tass).*
   We need (some cups/ some more cups).

4. Quand les poubelles sont-elles ramassées?
   *Kong lay poo-**bell** sonn-**tell** ra-**mass**ay?*
   When is the rubbish collected?

5. Pourrais-je emprunter –?
   *Pooray zhong-**prun**tay –?*
   Could I borrow –?

Thanks

Merci pour votre aide. Je vous suis très reconnaissant.*
*Mair-**see** poor votr **edd**. Zhuh voo swee tray rukkon-**ess**onn.*
Thank you for your help. I'm extremely grateful.

*reconnaissante *(..ess-**ont**)* if you're fema

Problems

un Entrepreneur
*uhn ontraprun-**ur***
a Builder

un Menuisier
*uhn mun-**weez**yay*
a Carpenter

un Électricien
*uhn aylek-treess-**yang***
an Electrician

un Plombier
uhn plombyay
a Plumber

− est bloqué
ay blokkay
− is Blocked

− est cassé
ay kassay
− is Broken

− est parti
*ay par-**tee***
− has Come Off

− est fendu
*ay fon-**duw***
− is Cracked

− fuit
fwee
− is Leaking

− est desserré
*ay des-**serr**ay*
− is Loose

− ne fonctionne pas
*nuh fonks-**yonn** pa*
− doesn't Work

. Pouvez-vous me montrer comment ça marche?
*Poovay-voo muh montray kommon sa **marsh**?*
　Can you show me how this works?

. Il y a un trou (dans le toit).
*Eel-**ya** uhn troo (don luh twa).*
　There's a hole (in the roof).

. Combien de temps cela prendra-t-il?
*Komb-**yang** duh tom sulla prondra teel?*
　How long will it take?

. Pouvez-vous recommander...
*Poovay-voo rukka-**monn**day...*
　Can you recommend...

3. Pouvez-vous le réparer?
*Poovay-voo luh ray-**parr**ay?*
　Can you mend it?

5. Combien ça va coûter?
*Komb-**yang** savva kootay?*
　What will it cost?

　... quelqu'un qui peut réparer − ?
*...kellkurn kee puh ray-**parr**ay −?*
　... someone who can mend −?

uand pourrez-vous le faire?
ong pooray-vous le faire?
　When can you do it?

When?

a n'est pas nécessaire (aujourd'hui/maintenant). (Demain/plus tard) serait parfait.
*a naypa naysess-**air** (oh-zhoord-**wee**/mantnong). (Duh-mang/pluw **taar**) surray parfay.*
　It doesn't need to be done (today/now). (Tomorrow/later) will be fine.

				la TRINGLE à RIDEAUX *la trangla-**ree**do* the Curtain Rail
un FAUTEUIL *uhn foh-**tay*** an Armchair	le PLAFOND *luh plaffong* the Ceiling	le PLACARD *luh plakkaar* the Cupboard	les RIDEAUX *lay reedo* the Curtains	
la CHEMINÉE *la shummy-**nay*** the Fire	le SOL *luh soll* the Floor	les VOLETS *lay vollay* the Shutters	les ESCALIERS *lay zes-**kal**yay* the Stairs	la FENÊTRE *la fuh-**netr*** the Window

The bedroom – *la chambre à coucher* – *la shombra koosha*

le LIT *luh lee* the Bed	une COUVERTURE *uwn koovair-**tuwr*** a Blanket	une COUETTE *uwn kwet* a Duvet	une LAMPE *uwn lomp* a Lamp	la LUMIÈRE *la luwm-**yair*** the Light
une AMPOULE *uwn om-**pool*** a Light Bulb	un OREILLER *uhn or-**ray**ay* a Pillow	une TAIE d'OREILLER *uwn tay dor-**ray**ay* a Pillowcase		les DRAPS *lay dra* the Sheets

le BAIN
luh bang
the Bath

la PRISE pour RASOIR
la preez poor razwaar
the Shaving Point

la CHAUDIÈRE
*la shohd-**yair***
the Boiler

la DOUCHE
la doosh
the Shower

le CHAUFFAGE CENTRAL
*luh shoh-**fazh** sonn-**tral***
the Central Heating

le ROBINET
luh robbynay
the Tap/Faucet

le LAVABO
luh lavvabo
the Washbasin

un FUSIBLE
*uhn fuw-**zeebl***
a Fuse

une SERVIETTE
*uwn sairv-**yet***
a Towel

la BOÎTE à
FUSIBLES
*la bwatt a fuw-**zeebl***
the Fuse Box

une BOUTEILLE de
GAZ
*uwn boo-**tay** duh
gaz*
a Gas Bottle

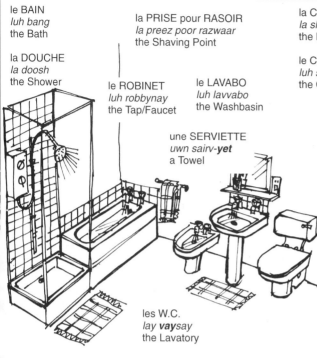

les W.C.
*lay **vay**say*
the Lavatory

le COMPTEUR
*luh komp-**tur***
the Meter

la VEILLEUSE
*la vay-**urz***
the Pilot Light

EAU chaude (froide)
oh shohd (frwad)
hot (cold) Water

le CHAUFFE-EAU
*luh shoh-**foh***
the Water Heater

un TUYAU
uhn twee-yo
a Pipe

Gas/electrics/plumbing

1. Il y a une fuite (de gaz/ d'eau).
   *Eel-**ya** uwn fweet (duh gaz/ doh).*
   There's a (gas/ water) leak.

2. (Fermer/ Ouvrir) le gaz/ l'eau.
   *(Fairmay/ Oov-**reer**) luh gaz/ loh.*
   Turn the gas/ water (Off/ On).

3. Il n'y a plus de gaz.
   *Eelnee-ya **pluw** duh gaz.*
   The gas has run out.

4. Il n'y a pas (d'eau chaude).
   *Eelnee **yapp**a (doh shohd).*
   There's no (hot water).

5. Est-ce que l'électricité est comprise?
   *Esskuh laylek-**trees**eetay ay kom-**preez**?*
   Is electricity included?

la PRISE de
COURANT
*la preez duh
koorong*
the (electric) Plug

la PRISE de
COURANT (femelle)
*la preez duh
koorong (fuh-**mell**)*
the Socket

le ROBINET
d'ARRÊT
*luh robbynay darr-**ay***
the Stopcock

l'INTERRUPTEUR
*lantairup-**tur***
the Light Switch

les Appareils Ménagers
the Appliances

le LAVE-VAISSELLE
*luh lavv ves-**sell***
the Dishwasher

le CONGÉLATEUR
*luh kong-zhayla-**tur***
the Freezer

le FRIGO
luh freego
the Fridge

un SÈCHE-CHEVEUX
*uhn sesh shuh-**vur***
a Hair Drier

un FER à REPASSER
*uhn fair a ruh-**pass**ay*
an Iron

le MICRO-ONDES
luh meekro awnd
the Microwave

la CUISINIÈRE
*la kweezeen-**yair***
the Stove

la TÉLÉ/ TÉLÉVISION
*la taylay/ -**veez**yong*
the TV

l'ANTENNE de TÉLÉ
*lonn-**tenn** duh taylay*
the TV Aerial

l'ASPIRATEUR
*laspeera-**tur***
the Vacuum Cleaner

la VIDÉO
*la **vee**day-o*
the Video

le LAVE-LINGE
*luh lavv **lanzh***
the Washing Machine

une CASSEROLE
*uwn kass-**rol***
a Saucepan

une SOUCOUPE
*uwn soo-**koop***
a Saucer

l'ÉVIER
***lay**vee-ay*
the Sink

une CUILLÈ
uwn kwee-y
a Spoon

Cutlery, crockery, etc.

un BOL
uhn boll
a Bowl

une CHAISE
uwn shezz
a Chair

la CAFETIÈRE/ THÉIÈRE
la kaffty-air/ tay-air
the Coffee pot/ Teapot

une TASSE
uwn tass
a Cup

la POUBELLE
la poo-bell
the Dustbin

une PELLE et un BALAI
uwn pell ay uhn bal-lay
a Dustpan and Brush

une SERPILLIÈRE
uwn sairp-yair
a Floorcloth

une FOURCHETTE
uwn foor-shet
a Fork

une POÊLE
uwn pwal
a Frying Pan

un VERRE
uhn vair
a Glass

un POT (à eau)
uhn poh (a oh)
a (water) Jug

un COUTEAU
uhn kooto
a Knife

BLE
bl
able

une PETITE CUILLÈRE
uwn puh-teet kwee-yair
a Teaspoon

un TORCHON
uhn torshong
a Tea Towel

une ASSIETTE
uwn ass-yet
a Plate

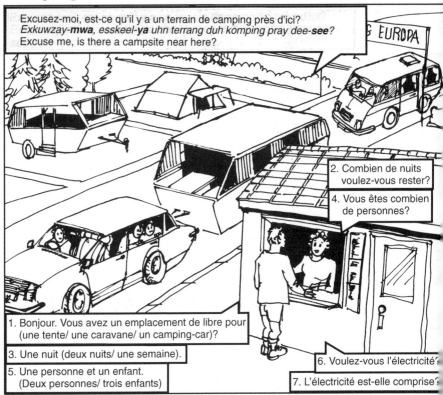

Excusez-moi, est-ce qu'il y a un terrain de camping près d'ici?
*Exkuwzay-**mwa**, esskeel-**ya** uhn terrang duh komping pray dee-**see**?*
Excuse me, is there a campsite near here?

2. Combien de nuits voulez-vous rester?

4. Vous êtes combien de personnes?

1. Bonjour. Vous avez un emplacement de libre pour (une tente/ une caravane/ un camping-car)?

3. Une nuit (deux nuits/ une semaine).

5. Une personne et un enfant.
(Deux personnes/ trois enfants)

6. Voulez-vous l'électricité?

7. L'électricité est-elle comprise?

1. *Bong-zhoor.Voo-**zavv**ay uhn om-**plas**mong duh leebr poor (uwn tont/ uwn kara-**van**/ uhn komping kaar)?*
   Hello. Have you a pitch for (a tent/ caravan/ motor caravan)?

2. *Komb-yang duh **nwee voo**lay-voo restay?*
   How long would you like to stay?

3. *Uwn nwee (dur nwee/ uwn suh-**men**).*
   One night (two nights/ a week).

   une (Bouteille/ Cartouche) de Gaz
   *uwn (boo-**tay**/ kar-**toosh**) duh gaz*
   a Gas (Cylinder/ Cartridge)

4. *Voo-**zet** komb-yang duh pair-**sonn**?*
   How many are there of you?

5. *Uwn pair-**sonn** ay uhn **on**fon.*
   *(Dur pair-**sonn**/ trwa-**zon**fon)*
   One person and one child.
   (Two people/ three children)

6. *__Voo__lay-voo laylek-**tree**seetay?*
   Would you like electricity?

7. *Laylek-**tree**seetay ettell kom-**preez**?*
   Is electricity included?

Campsite Signs		
Eau Potable	-	Drinking Water
Défense de Laver	-	No washing
Lavabos	-	Wash basins
Dames	-	Women
Hommes	-	Men
Vaisselle	-	Washing up
Poubelle	-	Dustbins
Vidoir de	-	Chemical Toilet
W.C. Chimiques		Disposal point

1. C'est combien par nuitée?
3. A quelle heure ferme-t-on les portes le soir?

2. Ça fait – francs. Vous avez un carnet?
4. A dix heures trente.

1. *Say komb-yang paar nweetay?*
   How much is it per night?

2. *Sa fay – frong. Voo-**zavv**ay uhn karnay?*
   That will be – francs. Have you a carnet?

3. *A kell-**ur fairm**-tonn lay port luh swaar?*
   What time do you close the gate in the evening?

4. *A deezur tront.*
   At 10.30.*

Taxe de séjour – tourist tax
   *Time p.53

Youth Hostel/Mountain Refuge

l'Auberge de Jeunesse
*loh-**bairzh** duh zhur-**ness***
the Youth Hostel

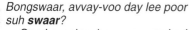

500 m

2. C'est pour combien de nuits?
4. Avez-vous des draps?

1. Bonsoir, avez-vous des lits pour ce soir?
3. Une nuit. Voici ma carte d'adhérent.

*Bongswaar, avvay-voo day lee poor suh **swaar**?*
   Good evening, have you any beds for tonight?

*Say poor komb-yang duh **nwee**?*
   How many nights?

*Uwn nwee. Vwa-**see** ma kaart da-**day**rong.*
   One night. Here's my membership card.

Avvay-voo day dra?
   Have you any sheets?

Meals *le petit déjeuner* – continental breakfast
le déjeuner – main meal, served 12 to 2 pm
le dîner – served 7.30 to 9 or 10 pm
Sunday lunch is the traditional time when French families eat out, so booking is advisable.

The Menu is called *La Carte*, *Un menu* is a set meal at a fixed price. Many restaurants offer several *menus: Je prends le menu à cent francs* – 'I'll have the 100 franc menu.' Within each set menu there is usually a choice, sometimes at extra cost *(en supplément)*. À *la carte* dishes are priced individually. A green salad frequently follows the main course.

Be prepared to keep your knife and fork if having several savoury courses.

You will often be asked – *Vous avez choisi?* – 'Have you decided/chosen?' – and *Vous avez terminé?* – 'Have you finished?'

Tipping: coffee/snacks 5-10%   meals 5-10%

Bars and cafés: it is cheaper to drink at the bar, but you should not order and pay there and then sit at a table.

Basics

Un (une), s'il vous plaît.
*uhn (uwn), seelvoo-**play***
A – please.

Cette place, est-elle occupée?
*set plass, ett-ell **okk**uwpay*
Is this seat/table taken?

Encore un (une), s'il vous plaît.
*ongkor **uhn** (uwn), seelvoo-**play***
Another one, please.

L'addition, s'il vous plaît.
*la-**dees**yong, seelvoo-**play***
Could I have the bill?

> A votre santé!   Bon appétit!   J'ai faim/ soif.
> *a votr sontay*   *bon appay-**tee***   *zhay fam/ swaff*
> Cheers!   Enjoy your meal!   I'm hungry/ thirsty.

un Couteau   une Fourchette   une Cuillère   un Verre   une Tasse
uhn kooto   *uwn foor-**shet***   *uwn kwee-**yair***   *uhn vair*   *uwn tass*
a Knife   a Fork   a Spoon   a Glass   a Cup

1. Bonjour, m'sieur-dame. Vous désirez?

4. Nous avons des sandwichs au (jambon) et au <u>fromage</u>.

2. Bonjour. Une pression, un milkshake et un citron pressé, s'il vous plaît.

3. Qu'est-ce que vous avez comme sandwichs?

*Bong-zhoor, musyuh-**dam**. Voo day-**zee**ray?*
Hello, [sir & madam] what would you like?

*Bong-zhoor. Uwn pressyong, uhn milkshake ay uhn seetrong pressay, seelvoo-**play**.*
Hello. A draught beer, a milkshake and a fresh lemon juice, please.

*Keskuh voo-**zavv**ay kom son-**veech**?*
What sandwiches have you got?

*Noo-**zavv**ong day son-**veech** oh (zhombong) ay oh <u>frommazh.</u>*
We have (ham) and <u>cheese</u> sandwiches.

Café	un Crème	un Déca	un Thé	au Lait (Citron)
*n kaff-**ay***	*uhn krem*	*uhn dayka*	*uhn tay*	*oh lay (see-trong)*
Black Coffee	a White Coffee	Decaffeinated	a Tea	with Milk (with Lemon)

Coca	un Coca Allégé/ Light	un Jus d'Orange	avec des Glaçons
n coca	*...a-**lay**zhay/ lite*	*uhn zhuw dor-**onzh***	*avvek day glassong*
Coke	a Diet Coke	an Orange Juice	with Ice

Verre de Vin (Rouge/Blanc)
n vair duh vang (roozh/blong)
Glass of (Red/White) Wine

une Bière (bière Blonde)
*uwn bee-**yair** (b.blawnd)*
a Beer (Lager)

un Croque-Monsieur
*uhn krock mus-**yuh***
Toasted Cheese & Ham Sandwich

1. Qu'est-ce que c'est?
2. Je voudrais un peu de cela, s'il vous plaît.
3. Et comme légumes?
4. Ceux-ci et ceux-là.

1. *Kesskuh **say**?*
   What's that?
2. *Zhuh voodray uhn pur duh sul-**la**, seelvoo-**play**.*
   I'd like some of that, please.

3. *Ay kom lay-**guwm**?*
   Which vegetables?
4. *Sur-**see** ay sur-**la**.*
   These and those.

Paying, the lavatory

1. Merci. Ça fait combien?
2. Excusez-moi, où sont les toilettes?

1. *Mair-**see**. Saffay komb-yang?*
   How much is that?

2. *Exkuwzay-**mwa**, oo song lay twa-**let***
   Excuse me, where are the toilets?

> 1. Bonjour, (monsieur/ madame).
>
> 2. Bonjour. (Je voudrais/ nous voudrions) prendre le petit déjeuner, s'il vous plaît
>
> 3. Pourrais-je avoir –, s'il vous plaît?

*Bong-zhoor, (mus-**yuh**/ ma-**dam**).*
Good morning, (sir/ madam).

*Bong-zhoor. (Zhuh voodray/ noo **voo**dree-ong) prondr luh putty **day**zhurnay, seelvoo-**play**.*
Good morning. (I'd like/ we'd like) breakfast, please.

*Pooray zhav-**waar** – , seelvoo-**play**?*
Could I have –, please?

déjeuner complet – full breakfast:

Chocolat
*n **shokk**ola*
Hot Chocolate

un (deux) Crème/s
uhn (dur) krem
one (two) White Coffee/s

un Croissant
uhn krwassong
a Croissant

du Lait
duw lay
some Milk

Chaud/Froid
shoh/frwa
Hot/Cold

Pain/ des Petits Pains
v pang/ day putty pang
ne Bread/ some Rolls

du Beurre
duw bur
some Butter

de la Confiture
*dulla kongfee-**tuwr***
some Jam

1. *Zhuh voodray **ray**zairvay uwn taabl poor (suh **swaar**/ deemonsh).*
   I'd like to book a table for (this evening/ Sunday).
2. *Poor kattr pair-**sonn**, a meedee ay duh-**mee**.*
   For (four), at 12.30.*
3. *A kell nom, mus-**yuh**?*
   What name, sir?

*Time p.53, phone p.51, days p.9

1. *Bong-zhoor (bong-swaar). Avvay-voo uwn taabl poor (dur/ trwa) pair-**sonn**?*
   Hello (good evening). Have you a table for (two/ three)?
2. *Uhn mohmong... Avvay-voo **ray**zairvay?*
   Just a moment... Have you booked?

* à point – *a pwang*	– medium
au poivre – *oh pwaavr*	+ peppercorns
bien cuit – *byang kwee*	– well done
bleu – *bluh*	– almost raw
frites – *freet*	– with chips
saignant – *senyong*	– rare

3. Vous désirez autre chose?

4. Vous désirez un dessert?

5. Cela vous a plu?

1. Je prends le menu à – francs, s'il vous plaît.

2. Un bifteck* pour moi – et des filets de poisson pour moi.

6. C'était très bon, merci.

*Zhuh pron luh muh-**nuw** a – frong, seelvoo-**play**.*
I'll have the – franc menu, please. [the set menu]

*Uhn **beef**tekk poor **mwa** – ay day feelay duh pwassong poor **mwa**.*
The steak* for me – and the fish fillets for me.

*Voo day-**zee**ray ohtr shohz?*
Would you like anything else?

*Voo day-**zee**ray uhn dess-**air**?*
Would you like dessert?

*Sul-**la** vooza **pluw**?*
Did you enjoy it?

*Saytay tray bong, mair-**see**.*
That was very nice, thank you.

e also Problems & queries, p. 28

1. Avez-vous des plats végétariens?

2. Est-ce qu'il y a (de la viande/ des noix) dedans?

3. Vous faites des portions pour enfants?

1. *Avvay-voo day **pla** vayzhaytarry-**ang**?*
   Have you any vegetarian dishes?

2. *Eskeel-**ya** (dulla vee-**ahnd**/ day **nwa**) duh-**dong**?*
   Has it got (meat/ nuts) in?

3. *Voo **fet** day porss-yong poor **on**fon?*
   Do you do children's portions?

4. Ce n'est pas ce que j'ai commandé. J'ai commandé – .

5. Pourriez-vous faire cuire ceci un peu plus, s'il vous plaît?

6. C'est sale.

7. Ça sent mauvais.

8. Ce n'est pas bon.

4. *Suh naypa sukkuh zhay kom-**monn**day. Zhay kom-**monn**day –.*
   This isn't what I ordered.
   I ordered –.

5. ***Poo**ree-ay voo fair kweer sus-**see** uhn pur **pluw**, seelvoo-**play**?*
   Could you cook this a bit more, please?

6. *Say sal.*
   This is dirty.

7. *Sa sonn mohvay.*
   This smells bad.

8. *Suh naypa bong.*
   This is bad.

9. L'addition, s'il vous plaît.

10. Je crois qu'il y a une erreur dans l'addition.

9. *La-**dees**yong, seelvoo-**play**.*
   Could I have the bill, please?

10. *Zhuh krwa keel-**ya** uwn er-**rur** don la-**dees**yong.*
   I think there's a mistake in the bill.

Ordering drinks

1. Que desirez-vous comme boisson?

3. Gazeuse ou plate?

2. Une carafe de vin (rouge/ blanc) et une bouteille d'eau minérale, s'il vous plaît.

1. *Kuh day-**zee**ray voo kom bwassong?*
   What would you like to drink?

2. *Uwn ka-**raff** duh vang (roozh/ blong) ay uwn boo-**tay** doh meenay-**ral**, seelvoo-**play**.*
   A carafe of (red/ white) wine and a bottle of mineral water, please.

3. *Gaz-**urz** oo platt?*
   Fizzy or still?

Ice cream – *une glace* – *uwn glass*

2. Quel parfum voulez-vous?

4. Une simple ou une double?

1. Avez-vous des glaces?

3. Une glace au chocolat.

au Cassis
oh kas-seece
Blackcurrant

au Chocolat
*oh **shokk**ola*
Chocolate

à la Pistache
*alla pee-**stash***
Pistachio

à la Fraise
alla frezz
Strawberry

à la Vanille
*alla van-**nee***
Vanilla

1. *Avvay-voo day **glass**?*
   Have you any ice cream?

2. *Kell par-**fung** voolay-voo?*
   What flavour would you like?

3. *Uwn glass oh **shokk**ola.*
   A chocolate ice cream.

4. *Uwn sampl oo uwn doobl?*
   One scoop or two?

boeuf
veau
beef

agneau
mouton
lamb

coq, poule(t), volaille
canard, dindon
poultry/game

porc
jambon
pork/ham

General terms

boisson comprise	drink included
la carte	menu
au choix	to choice
sur commande	prepared to order
couvert	cover charge
à emporter	take-away
entrée	first course
entremet	cream dessert
formule	limited menu
fumeur/non-fumeur	smoker/non-smoker
garniture au choix	choice of vegetables
menu – à prix fixe	set menu
– gastronomique	local specialities; gourmet
midi	lunch time
ou	or
à partir de	from
plat (du jour)	(today's) main dish
service – compris	service – included
– non compris/en sus	- extra
en supplément	extra charge

✳ ✳ ✳

à l'ANCIENNE	traditional recipe
à l'anglaise	boiled
abricots	apricots
agneau	lamb
aiglefin	haddock
ail	garlic
aïoli	garlic mayonnaise
airelles	cranberries
allégé	light
amandes	almonds
américaine	in white wine, cognac, tomatoes
ananas	pineapple
anchois; anchoïade	anchovies; paste or sauce
andouille, andouillette	tripe sausage
anguille – à l'étuvée	eel – stewed
– fumée	- smoked
arachide	peanut (uncooked)
arlésienne	& tomatoes, onions, aubergines, potatoes, rice

artichaut	artichoke
asperges	asparagus
assiette	plate
– anglaise	– assorted cold meat
aubergine	aubergine/eggplant
auvergnat	& cabbage, sausage bacon
avocat	avocado
BABA au rhum	rum baba
bar	bass
barbue	brill
basilic	basil
baudroie	monkfish
bavarois	moulded cream & custard dessert
bavette à l'échalote	beef with shallots
béarnaise	egg yolk, white wine shallot, vinegar sauce
bécasse	woodcock
béchamel	white sauce
beignet	doughnut/fritter
bercy	butter, white wine, shallot sauce
betterave	beetroot
beurre	butter
– blanc	– butter, white wine, vinegar sauce
– maître d'hôtel	– with parsley
bifteck	steak
bigarade	orange sauce
bijoux	choux pastries
biologique	organic
biscotte	rusk/thin toast
bisque	seafood soup
blanc	white; breast
blanquette – de veau	veal in white sauce
– de volaille	– chicken in white sauce & mushrooms
blettes	spinach beet
boeuf	beef
– à la mode	– with red wine & vegetables

bourguignon	– with red wine & mushrooms
en daube	– with red wine & herbs
es bois	wild
oisson	drink
sans alcool	– non-alcoholic
olets	boletus mushrooms
ombe	moulded ice cream dessert
onne femme	mushrooms, bacon, potatoes, onions
ordelaise	with red wine & vegetables
ouchée à la reine	chicken vol-au-vent
oudin blanc/noir	white/black pudding
ouillabaisse	fish soup/stew
ouilli	boiled
ouillon	broth/stock
oulangère	with potatoes & onions
oulettes	meatballs
ourgeoise	with carrots, onions, bacon, celery
ourguignonne	& red wine, onions, bacon, mushrooms
ourride	fish stew
andade de morue	poached, salt cod with potato
ebis	ewe's milk cheese
ème	bream
bresse	from Bresse
ik à l'oeuf	fried pastry with egg inside
ioche	sweet bun/large tea cake
ochet	pike
ochette	kebab
ocoli	broccoli
ugnon	nectarine
lot	whelk
ABILLAUD	cod
ori	kid
cahouètes	peanuts
ille	quail
ke	fruit/Dundee cake
mar	squid
campagne	country style
r canapé	on toast, canapé
nard	duck
érigourdin	– & prunes, goose livor pâté, truffles
neton	duckling
ores	capers
bonnade de boeuf	beer-braised beef
otte	carrot
ré	rack/loin of lamb
pe	carp
relet	plaice

cassis	blackcurrant/s
cassoulet	haricot bean, mutton, pork, goose, sausage stew
céleri	celery
céleri-rave	celeriac
cèpes	large mushrooms
cerf	venison
cerises	cherries
cervelas	saveloy – pork sausage
cervelle	brains
champignons	mushrooms
– à la grecque	– oil, herbs, tomato
– de Paris	– cultivated
chanterelles	wild golden mushrooms
charcuterie	assorted cold meat
chasseur	white wine, mushrooms, shallots
châtelaine	with artichoke hearts, chestnut purée
châteaubriand	large fillet steak
chaud	hot
chaud-froid	cold, jellied
chauffé	heated
chausson (aux pommes)	(apple) turnover
chèvre	goat
chevreuil	venison
chicorée	chicory, endive
chips	crisps
chou (rouge)	(red) cabbage
choucroute garnie	sauerkraut with sausage, smoked bacon
chou-fleur	cauliflower
choux de Bruxelles	Brussels sprouts
citron (vert)	lemon (lime)
citrouille	pumpkin
civet	game stew (jugged)
clafoutis	cherry flan made with batter
cochon	pig
coeurs d'artichaut	artichoke hearts
coing	quince
colin	coley
compote	stewed fruit
concombre	cucumber
confit	preserved goose or duck
consommé	clear soup
contrefilet	sirloin roast
coq au vin	chicken in red wine, bacon, onions, mushrooms
coquelet	cockerel
coques	cockles
coquillages	shellfish
coquilles St-Jacques	scallops in shells, cream sauce

cornichons	gherkins
côte	rib, chop
– de porc	– pork
– de veau	– veal
côtelette	chop
coulis	purée-like sauce
coupe – de fruits	bowl – of fruit salad
– glacée	– ice cream sundae
courgette	courgette/zucchini
couscous	bulgur wheat with spicy meat & vegetables
crabe	crab
crème	cream
– anglaise	– custard
– brûlée	– caramel custard, molten sugar topping
– chantilly	– whipped, sweetened
– fouettée	– whipped
– fraîche	– sour
– pâtissière	– confectioner's custard
crêpe	pancake
crépinette	small, highly seasoned sausage
cresson	watercress
crevettes – grises	shrimps
– roses	– prawns
croque-monsieur	toasted ham & cheese sandwich
– madame	– above with fried egg
croustade	in pastry shell
en croûte	wrapped in pastry
cru	raw
crudités	assorted raw vegetables
crustacés	fish, seafood
cuisse; cuissot	leg; haunch (venison)
cuit	cooked
DARNE	fish steak
dattes	dates
daube	stew
daurade	sea bream
diable	with strong mustard sauce
dinde, dindon/-neau	turkey
doux	sweet, mild
douzaine	dozen
duxelles	fried mushrooms & shallots with cream
ÉCHALOTE	shallot
écrevisse	crayfish
églefin	haddock
emballé	wrapped
endive	chicory/endive
entrecôte	rib steak
épaule	shoulder
éperlan	whitebait
épinards	spinach
escalope – milanaise	escalope – with tomato sauce
– panée	– breaded
escargot	snail
espadon	swordfish
estouffade	stew
estragon	tarragon
FAISAN	pheasant
farci	stuffed
faux-filet	sirloin
fenouil	fennel
au feu de bois	cooked on wood fire
feuilleté	puff pastry
fèves	broad beans
figues	figs
filet – de boeuf/porc	fillet – of beef/pork
fines herbes	mixed herbs
flageolets	small green kidney beans
flambé	flamed in alcohol
flamiche	leek tart
flétan	halibut
florentine	with spinach & cheese sauce
foie	liver
– gras	– duck/goose liver pâté
– de veau	– calf
– de volaille	– chicken
fond d'artichaut	artichoke heart
fondue	cheese fondue
– bourguignonne	– meat fondue
forestière	with bacon & mushrooms
au four	baked
fraîs/fraîche	fresh or chilled
fraises	strawberries
framboises	raspberries
frappé	iced
fricassée	rich cream sauce
frisée	curly endive
frit/e	fried
frites	chips/fries
friture	fried small fish
froid	cold
fromage/s	cheese
– blanc	– cream cheese
– frais	– soft cottage cheese
fruits de mer	seafood
fumé	smoked
GALANTINE	meat in aspic (usually chicken)
galette	wholewheat pancake
gambas	king prawns
garbure	thick cabbage soup
garni	with vegetables

âteau	cake	limande	lemon sole
aufre	waffle	lotte	monkfish
ermes de soja	bean sprouts	loup de mer	sea bass
ibier	game	lyonnaise	with onions
got (d'agneau)	leg (of lamb)		
ngembre	ginger	MACARON	macaroon
ace	ice cream	macédoine – de fruits	fruit salad
ougère	cheese-flavoured	– de légumes	– mixed vegetables
	choux pastry	madeleine	small sponge cake
oujons	small breaded meat or	madère	in Madeira
	fish pieces	magret (de canard)	(duck) breast
anite	type of sorbet	maïs	sweetcorn
gratin, gratiné	with cheese topping	maison	home-made
atin dauphinois	sliced potatoes baked	mandarine	tangerine
	in cream	maquereau	mackerel
enouille (cuisses de)	frogs' (legs)	marcassin	young wild boar
illades	grills	marmite	casserole
illé	grilled	– dieppoise	– creamy, curried fish
iottes	morello cherries		& seafood
oseilles	currants	marrons	chestnuts
		matelote	fish stew
ACHÉ	minced	médaillon	tenderloin steak
achis Parmentier	shepherd's pie	menthe	mint
reng	herring	merguez	spicy lamb sausage
ricots	beans	merlan	whiting
olancs	haricot beans	meunière	lightly floured, fried in
erts	green/French beans		butter
llandaise	sauce of egg yolks &	mijoté	stew
	butter	minceur	slimline
mard	lobster	moka	coffee flavoured
rs-d'oeuvres (variés)	(assorted) starters	morilles	morel mushrooms
ile	oil	mornay	in cheese sauce
d'arachide	– groundnut	morue	salt cod
d'olive	– olive	moules	mussels
le tournesol	– sunflower	– marinière	– & shallots in white
îtres	oysters		wine sauce
		mousse	mousse
S FLOTTANTES	soft meringues in	mousseline	mashed potato with
	custard		cream & eggs
		moutarde	mustard
MBON	ham	mouton	mutton
ru/cuit	– raw/cooked	mûres	blackberries
le Bayonne	– cured	museau de veau	brawn
bonneau	cured pig's knuckle	myrtilles	bilberries/blueberries
dinière	with mixed vegetables		
jour	of the day	NATURE	plain; 'neat' for drinks
enne	soup with shredded	navarin	stew
	vegetables	navet	turnip
	juice, gravy	niçoise	with garlic, olives,
			tomatoes
TUE	lettuce	noisettes	hazelnuts
gouste	crayfish	– d'agneau	– 'eye' of a lamb chop
goustines	scampi	noix	nuts/walnuts
gue	tongue	nouilles	noodles
in	rabbit		
, lardons	diced bacon	OEUF/S	egg/s
umes	vegetables	– brouillés	– scrambled
tilles	lentils	– à la coque	– boiled
eois	iced coffee with	– mollet/dur/s	– soft/hard-boiled
	whipped cream	– à la neige	– soft meringues in
re	hare		custard

– sur le plat	– fried
– poché	– poached
– à la russe	– Russian
oie	goose
oignon	onion
– farcies/noires/vertes	– stuffed/black/green
omelette	omelette
– aux champignons	– mushroom
– aux fines herbes	– herb
– au fromage	– cheese
– nature	– plain
– norvégienne	– baked alaska
onglet	cut of beef
os, à moelle	bone, marrow~
oursin	sea urchin
PAIN	bread
– au chocolat	– chocolate filled roll
– d'épices	– gingerbread
– grillé	– toast
– de mie	– white sliced bread
palmier	heart-shaped caramelised puff pastry
palombe	wood pigeon
palourdes	clams
pamplemousse	grapefruit
pan bagnat	roll with salad, anchovies, olive oil
pané	breaded
en papillote	baked in paper or foil
parfait	frozen mousse, sometimes ice cream
parfum	flavour
parmentier	with potatoes
pâté	pâté
– de campagne	– coarse pork
– de foie	– goose liver
pâtes	pasta
pâtisserie	cake
pavé	thick slice
paupiette (de veau)	rolled stuffed slice (of veal)
pays d'auge	in cream & cider
paysanne	with potatoes and vegetables
pêche	peach
perche	perch
perdrix, perdreau	partridge
périgourdine	with foie gras, maybe truffles
persil, persillé	parsley
petits farcis	stuffed vegetables
petits pois	green peas
pieds de porc	pig's trotters
pigeon	pigeon
pignons	pine nuts
piment	red pepper
– fort	– chili
pintade, pintadeau	guinea fowl

pipérade	tomatoes, peppers with scrambled eggs
pissaladière	onion tart with black olives & anchovies
pistache	pistachio
pistou	garlic, basil, olive oil sauce
plateau (de fromages)	(cheese) board
plie	plaice
poché	poached
poêlé	pan-fried
poire	pear
– belle Hélène	– with ice cream & chocolate sauce
poireaux	leeks
pois chiches	chick peas
poisson	fish
poitrine	breast
poivre	pepper
poivron (vert/rouge)	pepper (green/red)
pomme	apple
pommes (de terre)	potatoes
– allumettes	– matchstick chips
– duchesse	– mashed, piped & baked
– frites	– chips/french fries
– mousseline	– mashed
– nature	– boiled, steamed
– nouvelles	– new
– vapeur	– steamed, boiled
porc	pork
au porto	with port
potage	thick vegetable soup
– bonne femme	– leek & potato soup
pot-au-feu	beef & vegetable stew
potée auvergnate	cabbage & meat soup or stew
potiron	pumpkin
poule au pot	chicken with vegetables
poulet	chicken
– basquaise	– in ham, tomato, pepper sauce
– chasseur	– in wine, mushroom tomato sauce
poulpe	octopus
poussin	spring chicken
praliné	with caramelised nuts
pré-salé	grazed on salt marshes
primeurs	spring vegetables
profiteroles	choux pastry filled with whipped cream
provençale	with tomatoes, onion garlic, herbs
prune	plum
pruneau	prune
QUENELLES de brochet	light pike dumplings in cream sauce

uetsche	damson	– à point	– medium
ueue de boeuf	oxtail	– au poivre	– with black pepper
		sucre, sucré	sugar, sweet
RÂBLE	saddle	suprème de volaille	chicken breast in
aclette	melted cheese,		cream sauce
	potatoes & pickles		
adis	radishes	TARTE	tart, flan
agoût	stew	– aux pommes	– apple
aie	skate	– tatin	– upside-down apple
aisins	grapes		tart
âpé	grated/shredded	tartine	slice of bread & butter
e la région	local speciality	terrine	pâté
eines-claudes	greengages	tête de veau	calf's head (in jelly)
eligieuse	chocolate or coffee	thon	tuna
	cream choux bun	timbale	ramekin
llettes	potted pork	tomate	tomato
s	sweetbreads	tournedos	thick fillet steak
z	rice	tourte	pie
gnons	kidneys	tripes	tripe
sbif	roast beef	– à la mode de Caen	– with calf's trotters,
ti	roasted		vegetables, cider
uget	red mullet	tripoux	mutton tripe
ulade	soufflé mixture, Swiss	trou normand	glass of Calvados
	roll style		(apple brandy)
			drunk between
AFRAN	saffron		courses, or apple
n saison	in season		& Calvados sorbet
alade	salad	truffe	truffle
composée/mixte	– mixed	truite	trout
niçoise	– with tuna, tomatoes,	turbot	turbot
	anchovies, olives		
russe	– diced vegetables in	VACHERIN glacé	ice cream & meringue
	mayonnaise		cake
verte	– green	à la vapeur	steamed
lé	salted; preserved in	veau	veal
	brine	velouté	cream of ~ soup
nglier	wild boar	venaison	venison
rdines	sardines	en verdure	with green vegetable
ucisse; saucisson	sausage; salami		garnish
umon	salmon	véronique	with grapes, wine,
uté	lightly fried		cream
voyarde	with gruyère cheese	viande	meat
c	dry	volaille	poultry
l	salt		
le	sole	YAOURT, yogourt	yogurt
bonne femme	– in white wine &		
	mushrooms		* * * *
rbet	water ice/sherbet		
ubise	onion & cream sauce	*ENGLISH-FRENCH*	
upe	soup	cold	froid
a l'oignon	– onion, topped with	fat	le gras
	cheese on toast	flour	la farine
au pistou	– potato, courgette,	gluten-free	sans gluten
	bean, herb	hot (spicy)	chaud (épicé)
aghettis	spaghetti	nuts	les noix
ea(c)k	steak (beef)	salt	le sel
ien cuit	– well done	sugar	le sucre
leu	– almost raw	too	trop
rites	– & chips/fries	wheat	le blé
aché	– minced; burger	with	avec
aignant	– rare	without	sans

OUVERT	*FERMÉ*	*Tous les jours sauf...*
Open	Closed	Every day except...

Groceries: look for **Alimentation, Épicerie** – or **le supermarché** (supermarket). The **hypermarché** (hypermarket) is often in the **Centre Commercial**. Many shops close a or part of Monday.

How to ask: Often you don't need to know the actual name, just point and say:

Un de ceux-là, s'il vous plaît.	or	Un peu de cela, s'il vous plaît.
uhn duh sur-la, seelvoo-play		*uhn pur duh sul-la, seelvoo-play.*
One of those, please.		Some of that, please.

* * *

Vous avez des (pommes)?	Des (pommes), s'il vous plaît.
voo-zavvay day (pom)?	*day (pom), seelvoo-play*
Have you any (apples)?	Some (apples), please.
C'est combien?	Une livre de (tomates)
say komb-yang?	*uwn leevr duh (tom-att)*
How much is it/are they?	A $1/2$ kilo of (tomatoes)
Combien?	Cent grammes
komb-yang?	*song gram*
How much/many?	100g ($3^1/2$ oz)
Grand, Petit	La moitié/Un demi
gron, puh-tee	*la mwatty-ay/uhn duh-mee*
Big, Small	Half
Ceci, Cela	Un morceau de –
sus-see, sul-la	*uhn morso duh –*
This one, That one	A piece of –
Encore un petit peu.	Une tranche de –
ong-kor uhn putty pur	*uwn tronsh duh –*
A little more.	A slice of –

Ça suffit?	Assez *(assay)*	Autre chose?
sa suw-fee?	Ça va *(sa va)* } That's enough.	*ohtruh shoze?*
Is that enough?	Ça suffit	Anything else?
la pièce	*du pays*	*en réclame*
Each	Local produce	Special offer
Entrée libre	Je regarde seulement.	Désolé...
No obligation to purchase	*zhuh ruh-gaard surlmong*	*dayzollay*
	I'm just looking.	Sorry, we
		haven't...

Note: Use the conversation pattern at the baker's for all kinds of shops. It is usual to say **Bonjour** on entering and **Au revoir** when you leave. **Complaints:** see p. 4

1. Bonjour, madame.

2. Bonjour madame. Qu'est-ce que vous désirez?

3. Du pain, s'il vous plaît.

4. Je voudrais un pain comme cela. Et deux croissants.

*Bong-zhoor, ma-**dam**.*
Good morning (madam).

*Duw pang, seelvoo-**play**.*
Some bread, please.

*Zhuh voodray uhn pang kom sul-**la**. Ay dur krwassong.*
I'd like a loaf like that one. And two croissants.

2. *Bong-zhoor, ma-**dam**. Kesskuh voo day-**zee**ray?*
Good morning (madam). What would you like?

les petits pains *(day putty pang)* some rolls   une baguette *(uwn bag-**get**)* a French stick
pain complet *(pang komplay)* wholemeal bread

2. Non, c'est tout. Ça fait combien?

4. Voilà.

1. Voilà. Et avec ça?

3. Ça fait – francs.

5. Merci. Au revoir, madame.

*Vwa-**la**. Ay avvek **sa**?*
There you are. Would you like anything else?

Nong, say too. Sa fay komb-yang?
No, that's all. How much is that?

Sa fay – frong.
That's – francs altogether.

*Vwa-**la**.*
There you are.

*Mair-**see**. Oh ruv-**waar**, ma-**dam**.*
Thank you. Goodbye (madam).

When buying **sweets or chocolates** (des bonbons/ chocolats) you will often be asked if they are for a present:

C'est pour offrir? *Say poor off-**reer**?* – If so, they will wrap them for you.

du RÔTI de BOEUF
duw roh-tee duh burf
some roast Beef

du POULET
duw poolay
some Chicken

des CÔTELETTES
day kot-let
some Chops

un CANARD
uhn kannaar
a Duck

des ESCALOPES
day zeska-lop
some Escalopes

de la VIANDE HACHÉE
dulla vee-ahnd ashay
some Mince

du GIBIER
duw zheebee-ay
some Game

de l'AGNEAU
dull-anyo
some Lamb

des VOLAILLES
day voll-eye
some Poultry

du LAPIN
duw lappang
some Rabbit

des TRIPES
day treep
some Tripe

du VEAU
duw voh
some Veal

Delicatessen

du BOUDIN
duw boodang
some Black Pudding

du PÂTÉ
duw pattay
some Pâté

du PIZZA
duw peetza
some Pizza

du PORC
duw por
some Pork

des RILLETTES
day ree-yet
some Potted Meat

une QUICHE
uwn keesh
a Quiche

des SAUCISSES
day soh-seece
some Sausages

de la MERGUEZ
dulla mair-gayz
spicy Lamb Sausa

du JAMBON
duw zhombong
some Ham

des CRUDITÉS
day kruwdeetay
some raw Vegeta

du SAUCISSON
duw sohseesong
Slicing Sausage

de l'ANDOUILLETTE
dull-ondwee-yet
some Tripe Sausage

du POISSON
duw pwassong
some Fish

des FRUITS de MER
day frwee duh mair
some Seafood

es ANCHOIS
ay-zonshwa
ome Anchovies

du CABILLAUD/ MORUE
duw kabby-yo/ mo-ruw
some Cod

du CRABE
duw krab
some Crab

de la LIMANDE
dulla lee-mahnd
some Lemon Sole

u HOMARD
uw ommar
ome Lobster

des MOULES
day mool
some Mussels

des HUÎTRES
dayz weetr
some Oysters

des CREVETTES
day kruh-vet
some Prawns

u SAUMON
uw sohmong
ome Salmon

es ESCARGOTS
ay zeskargo
ome Snails

u CALMAR
uw kalmar
ome Squid

Poissons – Fruits de Mer

e TRUITE
wn trweet
Trout

THON
uw tong
me Tuna

Weights and measures

Dry weights

Liquid measures

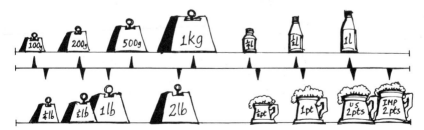

= 454g   1kg = 2lb 3oz   1L = 1 3/4 pts (Br.) = 2 pts 1$\frac{1}{2}$ fl.oz (US)

(in *English* order; French order in *Menu Guide*)

des CHAMPIGNONS
day shompeenyong
some Mushrooms

des POMMES de TERRE
day pom duh tair
some Potatoes

des ARTICHAUTS
day zarteesho
some Artichokes

des OLIVES
dayzoh-leev
some Olives

de la CHOUCROUTE
dulla shoo-kroot
some Sauerkraut

des ASPERGES
dayzas-pairzh
some Asparagus

des AUBERGINES
day zohbair-zheen
some Aubergines

un AVOCAT
uhn avvoka
an Avocado

des HARICOTS VERTS
day zarry-ko vair
some green Beans

un CHOU
uhn shoo
a Cabbage

des CAROTTES
day ka-rot
some Carrots

un CHOU-FLEUR
uhn shoo flur
a Cauliflower

du CÉLERI
duw sel-ree
some Celery

des COURGETTES
day koor-zhet
some Courgettes/Zucchini

un CONCOMBRE
uhn kawng-kawmbr
a Cucumber

de l'AIL
dull-eye
some Garlic

des POIREAUX
day pwarro
some Leeks

une LAITUE
uwn lay-tuw
a Lettuce

Je voudrais –
zhuh voodray –
I'd like –

un SAC
uhn sack
a Bag

des OIGNONS
day-zonyong
some Onions

des ÉPINARDS
day zaypeenaar
some Spinach

des PETITS POIS
day putty pwa
some Peas

du MAÎS
duw mah-eece
some Sweetcorn

un POIVRON
uhn pwaavrong
a Pepper

des TOMATES
day tom-att
some Tomatoes

les POMMES
lay pom
some Apples

des RAISINS
day rezzang
some Grapes

les ABRICOTS
lay zabbry-ko
some Apricots

un PAMPLEMOUSSE
uhn pompluh-moose
a Grapefruit

un MELON (une PASTÈQUE)
uhn mullong (uwn pas-tek)
a Melon (Watermelon)

des BRUGNONS
day bruwn-yong
some Nectarines

des ORANGES
dayzor-onzh
some Oranges

une PÊCHE
uwn pesh
a Peach

des POIRES
day pwaar
some Pears

un ANANAS
uhn anna-na
a Pineapple

des PRUNES
day pruwn
some Plums

des MIRABELLES
day meera-bell
small yellow Plums

des FRAMBOISES
day frongbwaz
some Raspberries

des GROSEILLES
day groh-zay
some Redcurrants

des FRAISES
day frez
some Strawberries

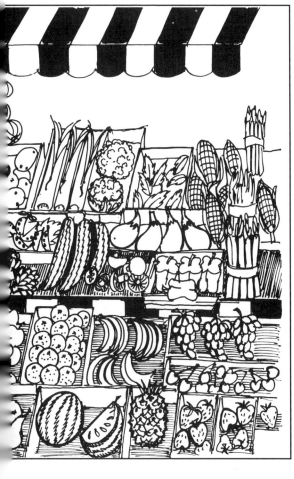

s BANANES
y bann-ann
me Bananas

des CERISES
day suh-reez
some Cherries

un CITRON (C. VERT)
uhn seetrong (vair)
a Lemon (Lime)

(in *English* order)

> Je voudrais –
> *Zhuh voodray* –
> I'd like –

> Vous avez –?
> *Voo-**zavv**ay* –?
> Have you any – ?

de la BIÈRE
*dulla bee-**air***
some Beer

des PÂTES
day patt
some Pasta

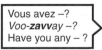

des BISCUITS
day biskwee
some Biscuits/Cookies

du PATÉ
duw pattay
some Pâté

du BEURRE
duw bur
some Butter

du RIZ
duw ree
some Rice

des CÉRÉALES
*day sayray-**al***
some Cereal

de la LESSIVE
*dulla les-**seev***
some Soap Powder

du FROMAGE (de chèvre)
duw frommazh (duh shevr)
some (goat's) Cheese

du SUCRE
duw suwkr
some Sugar

du CAFÉ
*duw kaff-**ay***
some Coffee

du THÉ
duw tay
some Tea

des OEUFS
*day-**zur***
some Eggs

du PAPIER HYGIÉNIQUE
*duw pappyay eezhee-ay**neek***
some Toilet Paper

du JUS de FRUITS
duw zhuw duh frwee
some Fruit Juice

du LIQUIDE pour la VAISSELLE
*duw lee-**keed** poor la ves-**sell***
some Washing-up Liquid

du MIEL
*duw mee-**ell***
some Honey

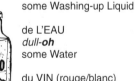

de L'EAU
*dull-**oh***
some Water

de la CONFITURE
*dulla kongfee-**tuwr***
some Jam

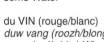

du VIN (rouge/blanc)
duw vang (roozh/blong)
some (red/white) Wine

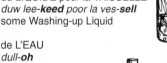

de la MARGARINE
*dulla margha-**reen***
some Margarine

du YAOURT
*duw ya-**oor***
some Yogurt

du LAIT (demi-/ écrémé)
*duw lay (dummy-/ ay-**kray**may)*
some (semi-/ skimmed) Milk

du SEL   du POIVRE
duw sell   duw pwaavr
some Salt   some Pepper

de L'HUILE
*dull **weel***
some Oil

de la MOUTARD
dulla moo-tard
some Mustard

Maison de la Presse-Journaux
Newspapers

Librairie-Papeterie
Bookshop-Stationery

un LIVRE
uhn leevr
a Book

un DICTIONNAIRE
*uhn deeksyon-**air***
a Dictionary
FRANÇAIS-ANGLAIS
fronsay-onglay
French-English

une PELLICULE pour
(photos papier/ diapositives)
*uwn pelly-**kuwl***
a Film for (prints/ slides)

un CRAYON
uhn krayong
a Pencil

un STYLO
uhn steelo
a Pen

n JOURNAL (anglais)
hn zhoor-nal (onglay)
n (English) Newspaper

une CARTE (ROUTIÈRE)
*uwn kaart (rooty-**air**)*
a (Road) Map

Tabac – Tobacconist

ne CARTE POSTALE
*wn kaart pos-**stal***
Postcard

un TIMBRE
uhn tambr
a Stamp

une PILE
uwn peel
a Battery

une LAMPE de POCHE
*uwn lomp duh **posh***
a Torch/Flashlight

des ALLUMETTES
*day-zalluw-**met***
some Matches

des CIGARETTES
*day seega-**ret***
some Cigarettes

un BRIQUET
uhn breekay
a Lighter

un DÉCAPSULEUR
*uhn day-kapsuw-**lur***
a Bottle Opener

(avec Filtre)
(avvek feeltr)
(with Filter)

un TIRE-BOUCHON
uhn teer booshong
a Corkscrew

un OUVRE-BOÎTES
*uhn oovr **bwatt***
a Tin/Can Opener

une AIGUILLE
*uwn ay-**gwee***
a Needle

du FIL
duw feel
some Thread

des CISEAUX
day seezo
some Scissors

de la FICELLE/CORDE
*dulla fee-**sell**/kord*
some String/Rope

The *Pharmacie* sells mainly drugs and medicines. Toiletries are sold at the *Droguerie*.
Service de garde/d'urgence or *pharmacie de service* – duty/emergency chemist.

> Je voudrais quelque chose pour – .
> *Zhuh voodray kellkuh shoze poor – .*
> I'd like something for – .

une Écorchure	une Piqûre d'Insecte	les Coups de Soleil	le Mal de Tête
*uwn aykor-**shur***	*uwn pee-**kuwr** dan-**sekt***	*lay koo duh sol-**lay***	*luh mal duh **tet***
a Graze	an Insect Bite	Sunburn	Headache

la Constipation	une Toux	la Diarrhée	les Douleurs d'Oreille
*la kongsty-**pas**yong*	*uwn too*	*la dee-a **ray***	*lay doo-**lur** dor-**ray***
Constipation	a Cough	Diarrhoea	Earache
le Rhume des Foins	le Mal de Mer	un Mal de Gorge	les Douleurs d'Eston
*luh ruwm day **fwang***	*le mal duh **mair***	*uhn mal duh **gorzh***	*lay doo-**lur** desto-ma*
Hay Fever	Sea Sickness	a Sore Throat	Stomach Ache

la Droguerie
Toiletries

Vous avez –?
*Voo-**zavv**ay –?*
Have you any –?

de l'ASPIRINE
*duh laspy-**reen***
some Aspirin

de la CRÈME ANTISEPTIQUE
*dulla krem onty-sep**teek***
some Antiseptic Cream

des ALIMENTS pour BÉBÉ
*day zally-mong poor **bay**bay*
some Baby Food

ne BANDE VELPEAU
*wn bond vel-**po***
Crepe Bandage

un PEIGNE
uhn penyuh
a Comb

des PRÉSERVATIFS
*day prayzairva-**teef***
some Condoms

du COTON
duw kottong
some Cottonwool

n DÉODORANT
*hn **day**-odorong*
Deodorant

de la CRÈME ANTI-INSECTE
*dulla krem onty-an**sekt***
some Insect Repellant

des COUCHES
day koosh
some
Nappies/Diapers

un RASOIR
uhn razzwaar
a Razor

es MOUCHOIRS en PAPIER
ay mooshwaar ong pappyay
me Paper Handkerchiefs

des PANSEMENTS
day poncemong
some Plasters/Band-Aid

du SAVON
duw savvong
some Soap

de la CRÈME à RASER
dulla krem a razzay
some Shaving Cream

es SERVIETTES HYGIÉNIQUES
*ay sairv-**yet** eezhee-ay**neek***
anitary Napkins/Towels
TAMPONS – *tompong* – Tampons)

du SHAMPOOING
*duw shom-**pwang***
some Shampoo

du DENTIFRICE
*duw donty-**freece***
some Toothpaste

des LUNETTES de SOLEIL
*day luw-**net** duh sol-**lay***
some Sunglasses

de l'HUILE SOLAIRE
*dull **weel** soll-**air***
some Suntan Oil

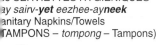

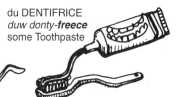

une BROSSE à DENTS
*uwn bross a **dong***
a Toothbrush

un CHAPEAU
uhn shappo
a Hat

un BONNET
uhn bonnay
a Woolly Hat

une CHEMISE (un T-SHIRT)
*uwn shuh-**meeze** (uhn tee shirt)*
a Shirt (a T-shirt)

une JUPE
uwn zhuwp
a Skirt

un SLIP
uhn sleep
Briefs/Underpants

une ROBE
uwn robb
a Dress

un MAILLOT (de bain)
uhn my-oh (duh bang)
a Swimming Costume/Trunks

des COLLANTS
*day **koll**ong*
some Tights

une VESTE
uwn vest
a Jacket

des CHAUSSETTE
*day shoh-**set***
some Socks

un PULL
uhn puwl
a Sweater

un MANTEAU
uhn monto
a Coat

un PANTALON (un JEAN)
uhn pontalong (uhn jean)
some Trousers (Jeans)

des CHAUSSURES
*day shoh-**suwr***
some Shoes

un SHORT
uhn short
some Shorts

des GANTS
day gonn
some Gloves

une CEINTURE
*uwn sang-**tuwr***
a Belt

un MOUCHO
uhn mooshwa
a Handkerchi

1. *Bong-zhoor. Zhuh voodray uwn shuh-**meeze**.*
   Hello. I'd like a shirt.

2. *Wee. Kell ay votr tie?*
   What size do you take?

3. *Zhuh fay duw kar-ront. Poovay-voo prahndr may muh-**zuwr**?*
   I take size 40. Can you measure me?

4. *Voo lavvay on (**blur**)?*
   Have you got it in (blue)?

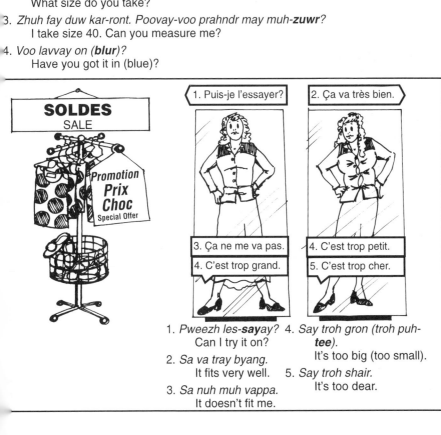

1. *Pweezh les-**say**ay?*
   Can I try it on?

2. *Sa va tray byang.*
   It fits very well.

3. *Sa nuh muh vappa.*
   It doesn't fit me.

4. *Say troh gron (troh puh-**tee**).*
   It's too big (too small).

5. *Say troh shair.*
   It's too dear.

1. *Je le prends. Ça fait combien?*
2. *Voulez-vous payer à la caisse?*
3. *Acceptez-vous les (cartes bancaires/ dollars/ travellers)?*
4. *Merci.*
5. *Je vous en prie.*

Caisse

1. *Zhuh luh pron. Sa fay komb-yang?*
   I'll take this one. How much is it?

2. *Voolay-voo payay alla **kess**.*
   Please pay at the cash desk.

3. *Ak-**sep**tay voo lay (kaart bong-**kair**/ doll-aar/ trav-**lair**)?*
   Do you take (credit cards/ dollars/ traveller's cheques)?

4. *Mair-**see**.*
   Thank you.

5. *Zhuh voozon **pree**.*
   Not at all.

Exchanges/complaints

1. *Pouvez-vous changer ceci?*
2. *Je voudrais faire une réclamation.*
3. *Pouvez-vous me rembourser?*
4. *Voici le reçu.*

1. *Poovay voo shonzhay sus-**see**?*
   Can you change this for me?

2. *Zhuh voodray fair uwn raykla-**mas**yong.*
   I want to make a complaint.

3. *Poovay voo muh rom-**boor**say?*
   Can you give me a refund?

4. *Vwa-**see** luh ray-**suw**.*
   Here's the receipt.

Cash dispenser:
Introduisez votre carte
Insert card
  Veuillez patienter
  Please wait
Composez votre numéro
Enter PIN number
  ...le montant désiré
  Enter amount required
Tapez 'fin'
Press 'fin' (end)
  Retirez votre carte
  Withdraw card

Currency: 1 franc = 100 centimes

un billet	de l'argent
uhn beeyay	*dull-**aar**zhong*
a note	some money

1. Où est-ce qu'il y a (un distributeur de billets/ une banque)?

2. C'est là-bas, sur la place.

. *Oo eskeel-**ya** (uhn distry-buw**tur** duh **bee**yay/ uwn bonk)?*
  Where will I find (a cash dispenser/ a bank)?

. *Say lab-**ba**, suwr la plass.*
  It's over there, in the square.

o change money look for *Change* sign

CAISSE

SONNER
Ring

2. Votre passeport, s'il vous plaît.

3. Voulez-vous signer ici.

4. Vous pouvez prendre l'argent à la caisse.

1. Je voudrais changer (des livres/ des dollars/ un travellers).

*Zhuh voodray shonzhay (day leevr/ day doll-aar/ uhn trav-**lair**).*
  I'd like to change (some pounds/ dollars/ a traveller's cheque).
*Votr passpor, seelvoo-**play**.*
  Your passport, please.
*Voolay-voo seenyay ee-**see**.*
  Please sign here.
*Voo poovay prondr laarzhong alla **kess**.*
  Collect the money from the cashier.

Où est le bureau de poste, s'il vous plaît?
*Oo-ay luh buwro duh **posst**, seelvoo-**play**?*
Where is the post office, please?

1. Vous vendez des timbres?

2. Pour (la Grande Bretagne/ les États-Unis), s'il vous plaît.

1. *Voo vonday day **tambr**?*   **Stamps** can also be bought at the **Taba**
   Do you sell stamps?

2. *Poor (la Grond Bruh-**tan**ya/ layzay **taz**uw-**nee**), seelvoo-**play**.*
   To (Gt. Britain/ USA), please.

French and Swiss post boxes are yellow, Belgian ones red.
Foreign mail may have a separate slot: *Etranger.*
Many post offices also change money – look for **Change** sign.

Public holidays – *Jours fériés*

F	New Year's Day	January 1	B/CH
		January 2	CH
F	Easter Monday		B/CH
F	Labour Day	May 1	B
F	Victory in Europe Day	May 8	
F	Ascension Day	40 days after Easter	B/CH
F	Whit Monday	7th after Easter	B/CH
F	Bastille Day	July 14	
	National Day	July 21	B
	National Day	August 1	CH
F	Assumption	August 15	B
F	All Saints' Day	November 1	B
F	Remembrance Day	November 11	B
F	Christmas Day	December 25	B/CH
	St Stephen's Day	December 26	CH

F – France   B- Belgium   CH – Switzerland

Telephone – *le téléphone*

> Où est le téléphone
> (le plus proche)?

*Oo-ay luh taylay-**fonn** (luh pluw prosh)?*
Where is the (nearest) phone?

> Puis-je utiliser votre
> téléphone?

*Pweezh uwtee-**lee**zay
votr taylay-**fonn**?*
Can I use your phone,
please?

> Une carte de téléphone,
> s'il vous plaît.

< 50 ou 120 unités?

*Uwn kaart duh taylay-**fonn**, seelvoo-**play**.*
A phone card, please.

*Sangkont oo son-**dur** oon**ee**tay?*
50 or 120 units?

If a phone box takes incoming calls, its
number is shown on top right of information
board.

1. Allô.

2. C'est – .

3. Je voudrais parler
à – , s'il vous plaît.

5. Je voudrais faire
un appel en PCV.

4. Ne quittez pas!

. *Allo.*
   Hello.

2. *Say – .*
This is – .

. *Zhuh voodray parlay a – , seelvoo-**play**.*
   Could I speak to – , please?

. *Nuh keetay **pa**!*
   Please hold.

Emergency numbers (free):
15 SAMU (Emergency Medical Services)
17 Police   18 Fire Brigade
Belgium: 101 Police
100 Fire & Ambulance
Luxembourg: all 012
Switzerland: 17 or 117 Police
118 Fire   144 Ambulance

Information: 12
European emergency services: 112
International operator: 00 33 plus your
country code
French telephone numbers are given in
twos: 12, 34, etc

Ringing home:
Dial 00, then your country code and local
code minus the first 0. To ring France from
abroad, omit the first 0 of the French code.

Britain dial	00 then	44
U.S. & Canada	00	1
Australia	00	61
New Zealand	00	64
Eire	00	353

Reduced rates apply 1900-0800 and at
weekends.

Most phones use *une **Télécarte***, sold at
tabacs, newsagents, post offices or station
kiosks. (British credit cards lack chips, so
do not work in French telephones.)

Instructions:

Décrochez	Lift receiver
Introduire la carte ou	Insert card or dial
faire le numéro d'urgence	emergency number
Patientez, s.v.p.	Please wait
Numérotez	Dial number
Retirez votre carte	Remove card

5. *Zhuh voodray fair uhn ap-**pell** on Pay Say **Vay**.*
I'd like to make a reverse-charge/collect call.

A	ah		**P**	pay
B	bay		**Q**	kuw
C	say		**R**	air
D	day		**S**	ess
E	uh		**T**	tay
F	eff		**U**	uw
G	zhay		**V**	vay
H	ash		**W**	doobluh vay
I	ee		**X**	eex
J	zhee		**Y**	eegrekk
K	kah		**Z**	zed
L	ell			
M	em		**é** aigu – *uh ayguw*
N	en		**è** grave – *uh grahv*
O	oh		**ê** circonflexe – *seerkongfle*

Comment ça s'écrit?	Pouvez-vous l'épeler?
*Kommon sa say-**kree**?*	*Poovay voo **lay**pullay?*
How do you spell that?	Can you spell it?

Taxi – *un taxi*

Tip: 10%

1. Où puis-je trouver un taxi?
2. Pouvez-vous appeler un taxi, s'il vous plaît?
3. A (l'aéroport/ la gare), s'il vous plaît.
4. A cette adresse, s'il vous plaît.
5. Ça coûtera combien?
6. Donnez-moi un reçu, s'il vous plaît.

1. ***Oo** pweezh troovay uhn taxi?*
   Where can I find a taxi?

2. *Poovay-voo applay uhn taxi, seelvoo-**play**?*
   Can you call a taxi, please?

3. *A (lairo-por/ la gaar), seelvoo-**play**.*
   To (the airport/ the station), please.

4. *A setta-**dress**, seelvoo-**play**.*
   To this address, please.

5. *Sa kooter-**ra** komb-yang?*
   How much will it cost?

6. *Donnay-mwa uwn rus-**suw**, seelvoo-**play**.*
   Could I have a receipt, please.

Time

12 noon – midi *(mee-dee)*
12 midnight – minuit
(meenwee)

Quelle heure est-il?
*Kell-**ur** ett-**eel**?*
What's the time?

Il est... une heure
*Eel ay... **uwn** ur*
It's... one o'clock

deux heures cinq
*dur-zur **sank***
five past two

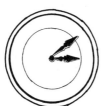

trois heures dix
*trwa-zur **deece***
ten past three

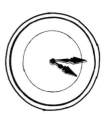

quatre heures et quart
*kattr ur ay **kaar***
quarter past four

cinq heures vingt
*sank ur **vang***
twenty past five

six heures vingt-cinq
*see-zur van-**sank***
twenty-five past six

sept heures et demie
*set-ur ay duh-**mee***
half past seven

huit heures moins vingt-cinq
*weet-ur mwang van-**sank***
twenty-five to eight

neuf heures moins vingt
*nurv-ur mwang **vang***
twenty to nine

dix heures moins le quart
*dee-zur mwang luh **kaar***
quarter to ten

onze heures moins dix
*awn-zur mwang **deece***
ten to eleven

midi moins cinq
*mee-dee mwang **sank***
five to twelve (noon)

Full-scale business negotiations are beyond the scope of this book. This section will enable you to negotiate the switchboard or reception desk, make appointments and leave messages. Some financial and product terms are also included.

May I speak to –?

1. *Pooray-zhuh parlay a (mus-**yuh**/ ma-**dam**) –, seelvoo-**play**?*
   May I speak to (Mr/ Ms) –, please?

2. *Kellay song nuwmayro duh **posst**?*
   What's his/her extension?

3. *Say luh – .*
   It's – .

4. *Nuh keetay **pa**, seelvoo-**play**.*
   Please hold.

5. *Luh posst ett **okk**uwpay.*
   It's engaged.

6. *Voo voolay at-**tondr**?*
   Do you want to hold?

1. Je voudrais parler au Directeur (Directeur Export/ Directeur des Ventes).

2. Quel est son nom?

3. Il faudrait parler à (Monsieur/ Madame) – à notre bureau de – .

4. Pouvez-vous me donner le numéro?

1. *Zhuh voodray parlay oh deerek-**tur** (deerek-**tur** ex-**por**/ deerek-**tur** day **vont**).*
   I'd like to speak to the manager (export/ sales manager).

2. *Kellay song nom?*
   What's his/her name?

3. *Eel fohdray parlay a (mus-**yuh**/ ma-**dam**) – a notr buwro duh – .*
   You need to speak to (Mr/Ms) – at our office in – .

4. *Poovay-voo muh donnay luh **nuw**mayro?*
   Can you give me the number?

Who's calling?

2. C'est de la part de – .

1. De la part de qui?

3. Pouvez-vous l'épeler?

4. Et le nom de votre société?

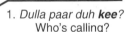

1. *Dulla paar duh **kee**?*
   Who's calling?

2. *Say dulla paar duh – .*
   This is – .

3. *Poovay-voo **lay**pullay?*
   Can you spell that, please?

4. *Ay luh nom duh votr **soss**-yaytay?*
   And the name of your company?

They're not available

3. Quand sera-t-il de retour?

4. Je rappellerai plus tard.

1. Il est absent en ce moment.

2. Je regrette, il est en réunion en ce moment.

1. *Eel-ett **ab**sonn onsuh mohmong.*
   He is not in at present.

2. *Zhuh rug-**ret**, eel **ett**-on ray-**uwn**yong onsuh mohmong.*
   I'm sorry, he's in a meeting at present.

3. *Kon surra-**teel** duh ruh-**toor**?*
   When do you expect him to be free?

4. *Zhuh rap-**pell**eray pluw taar.*
   I'll call back later.

Leaving a message

1. Puis-je laisser un message, s'il vous plaît?

3. Quel est votre numéro?

5. Je lui donnerai votre message.

2. Pouvez-vous lui demander de me rappeler?

4. C'est le (douze...trente-quatre...cinquante-six).

1. *Pweezh lessay uhn **mess**-azh, seelvoo-**play**?*
   Can I leave a message, please?

2. *Poovay-voo lwee duh-**monn**day dummuh **rapp**lay?*
   Could you ask him/her to ring me?

3. *Kellay votr **nuw**mayro?*
   What's your number?

4. *Say luh (dooz...tront-kattr...sangkont-seece).*
   It's (12.34.56).ᐞ

5. *Zhuh lwee donneray votr **mess**-azh.*
   I'll give him your message.

6. *Zhuh voo rummair-**see**.*
   Thank you very much.

7. *Duh ree-**ang**.*
   Not at all.

6. Je vous remercie.

7. De rien.

Nos p.112

1. Bonjour, (monsieur/ madame). Vous désirez?

2. J'ai rendez-vous avec (Monsieur/ Madame) – à 15 heures.

5. Je suis de – .

6. Voici ma carte de visite.

3. Oui (monsieur/madame). Votre nom, s'il vous plaît?

4. Et le nom de votre société?

1. *Bong-zhoor (mus-**yuh**/ ma-**dam**). Voo day-**zee**ray?*
   Good morning/afternoon (sir/ madam). Can I help you?

2. *Zhay ronday-**voo** avvek (mus-**yuh**/ ma-**dam**) – a kan-zur.*
   I have an appointment with (Mr/ Ms) – at 3 o'clock.

3. *Wee (mus-**yuh**/ ma-**dam**). Votr nom, seelvoo-**play**?*
   Certainly, (sir/ madam). Your name, please?

4. *Ayluh nom duh votr **soss**-yaytay?*
   And the name of your company?

5. *Zhuh swee duh – .*
   I represent – .

6. *Vwa-**see** ma kaart duh vee-**zeet**.*
   Here's my card.

1. Je voudrais prendre rendez-vous avec (Monsieur/ Madame) – .

2. ... de preference (le matin/ l'après-midi).

3. Je suis libre (demain/ lundi prochain/ le 4 mai).

4. (Il/ elle) pourrait vous recevoir (le mardi 11) à 15 heures.

5. Cela vous convient-il?

6. Je serai très heureux de vous rencontrer.

7. J'espère que nous pourrons faire des affaires ensemble.

1. *Zhuh voodray prondr ronday-**voo** avvek (mus-**yuh**/ ma-**dam**) – .*
   I'd like to make an appointment to see (Mr/ Ms) – .

2. *duh **pray**fayronss (luh mattang/ lappray **mee**dee).*
   ... preferably (in the morning/ in the afternoon).

3. *Zhuh swee leebr (duh-**mang**/ lurndee **prosh**ang/ luh kattr may).*
   I am free (tomorrow/ next Monday/ on 4 May).

4. *(Eel/ ell) pooray voo russuh-vwaar (luh mardee **awnz**) a kan-zur.*
   (He/ she) could see you on (Tuesday 11) at 3 o'clock.

5. *Suh-**la** voo konv-yang teel?*
   Is that convenient?

6. *Zhuh surray trayzur-**rur** duh voo ron-**kon**tray.*
   I look forward to meeting you.

7. *Zhes-**pair** kuh noo poorong fair dayzaf-**fair** on-**sombl**.*
   I hope we can do business together.

Finding the office (*le bureau* – *luh buwro*)

1. Prenez l'ascenseur jusqu'au troisième étage.

2. (Il/ elle) arrive.

1. *Prunnay lasson-**sur** zhuwsko tr-**waz**yem ay-**taazh**.*
   Take the lift to the third floor.

2. *(Eel/ ell) ar-**reev**.*
   (He/ she) is just coming.

1. *Zhuh swee trayzur-**rur** duh voo ron-**kon**tray.*
   I'm delighted to meet you.   **heureuse* if you're female

2. *Pweezh voo pray-**zon**tay mong kol-**leg**, (mus-**yuh**/ ma-**dam**) –?*
   May I introduce my colleague, (Mr/ Ms) –?

3. *Zhes-**pair** voo ruv-**waar** byangto.*
   I look forward to meeting you again.

4. *Oh ruv-**waar**, ay mair-**see** ong-**kor**.*
   Goodbye, and thank you again.

1. Avez-vous reçu (ma lettre/ mon fax/ mon email)?
   *Avvay-voo rus-**suw** (ma lettr/ mong fax/ mong **ee**mail)?*
   Have you received (my letter/ fax/ email)?

2. Serait-il possible d'envoyer un fax?
   *Surrett-eel pos-**seebl** donvw-**eye**-ay uhn fax?*
   Could I send a fax, please?

3. Quel est votre numéro de fax?
   *Kellay votr **nuw**mayro duh fax?*
   What's your fax number?

4. Quelle est votre adresse email?
   *Kellay votra-**dress ee**mail?*
   What's your email address?

5. J'aurais besoin de quelqu'un pour taper une lettre.
   Zhawray buzzwang duh kellkurn poor tappay uwn lettr.
   I need someone to type a letter for me.

6. Pourriez-vous photocopier ceci?
   *Pooree-ay voo foto**kop**-yay sus-**see**?*
   Could you photocopy this for me?

7. Puis-je utiliser votre téléphone?
   *Pweezh uwtee-**lee**zay votr taylay-**fonn**?*
   Could I use your phone?

8. Ça n'est pas nécessaire aujourd'hui/ maintenant. (Demain/ plus tard) serait parfait.
   *Sa naypa naysess-**air** (oh-zhoord-**wee**/mantnong). (Duh-mang/pluw **taar**) surray parfay.*
   It doesn't need to be done (today/ now). (Tomorrow/ later) will be fine.

9. Merci de votre aide. Je vous suis très reconnaissant.*
   *Mair-**see** duh votr **edd**. Zhuh voo swee tray rukkon-**ess**onn.*
   Thank you for your help. I'm extremely grateful.

   *reconnaissante (...ess-**ont**) if you're female

Office equipment

Ordinateur
*ordy-natt-**ur***
le Computer

une Disquette
*uwn dees-**ket***
a Disk

Logiciel
*sh lozheece-**yell***
le Software/Programme

un Rétroprojecteur
*uhn raytro-prozhek-**tur***
an Overhead Projector

Je cherche des renseignements sur – .
I'd like information about – .

Pouvez-vous m'envoyer une brochure et une liste de prix...
Could you send a brochure and a price list...

... pour des machines capables de traiter 200kg par heure?
... for machines capable of processing 200 kg/hour?

un Agent/ Représentant
*uhn **azh**ong/ ruppray-**zon**tonn*
an Agent/ Representative

une Succursale
*uwn suwkuwr-**sal***
a Branch

un Distributeur
*uhn deestreebuw-**tur***
a Distributor

le Siège Social
*luss **yezh** soss-**yal***
the Head Office

une Documentation
*uwn dokkuwmon-**tas**yong*
some Publicity Material

une Filiale
*uwn feel-**yal***
a Subsidiary

The product

la fabrication
the assembly

un lot (de produits)
a batch (of production)

le composant
the component

le produit
the product

la gamme
the product range

une nouvelle ligne
a new line

les matières premières
the raw materials

les produits finis
the finished products

la ligne de fabrication
the production line

au choix
of your choice

un bon de commande
an order form

passer une commande
to place an order

le contrat
the contract

attribuer un contrat
to award a contract

la date de livraison souhaitée
the delivery date requested

Finance

Nous accordons une remise de 30%.
We would allow a discount of 30%.

Notre chiffre d'affaires annuel est de (3 millions).
We have a turnover of (3 million) a year.

l'avance	un compte bancaire	
advance	a bank account	
une carte bancaire	un chèque	la commission
banker's card	a cheque	the commission
les frais	un devis	facturer
the costs	an estimate	to invoice
une facture (pro-forma)	en monnaie locale	un prix forfaitaire
a (pro-forma) invoice	in local currency	an inclusive price
un devis	le taux d'intérêt	un reçu
a quotation	the rate of interest	a receipt
un relevé de compte	hors taxes	le total
a statement of account	before tax	the total
faire un virement	TVA	par écrit
to make a transfer	VAT	in writing

le CENTRE-VILLE
*luh sontruh **veel***
the Town Centre

la PLAGE
la plazh
the Beach

le PONT
luh pong
the Bridge

la CATHÉDRALE
*la kattay-**dral***
the Cathedral

le CHÂTEAU
luh shatto
the Chateau

l'ÉGLISE
*lay-**gleez***
the Church

le CINÉMA
luh seenayma
the Cinema

la FÔRET
la forray
the Forest

l'HÔPITAL
*loppy-**tal***
the Hospital

l'ÎLE
leel
the Island

le LAC
luh lakk
the Lake

le PARC
luh paar
the Park

la ROUTE/ la RUE
la root/ la ruw
the Road/ Street

la PLACE du MARCHÉ
la plass duw marshay
the Marketplace

le POSTE de POLICE
luh posst duh police
the Police Station

les MAGASINS
lay magga-zang
the Shops

le MUSÉE
luh muwzay
the Museum

la RIVIÈRE
*la reev-**yair***
the River

la GARE (G.ROUTIÈRE)
*la gaar (g.rooty-**air**)*
the Station (Bus Station)

NORD
nor
North

OUEST
oo-est
West

EST
est
East

SUD
suwd
South

THÉÂTRE *…h tay-aatr* …e Theatre	la MAIRIE/l'HÔTEL de VILLE *la mair-ee/loh-tell duh veel* the Town Hall	le SYNDICAT (d'Initiative)/ l'OFFICE de TOURISME *luh sandy-ka/* *l'off-eece duh too-reezm* the Tourist Office
TUNNEL (sous la Manche) *…h tuw-nell (soo la monsh)* …e (Channel) Tunnel		
VALLÉE *… vall-ay* …e Valley		

Où se trouve? ***Oo suh troov?*** ⎱ Where is ?
Où est? ***Oo-ay?*** ⎰

Pour aller à – , s'il vous plaît?
*Poor allay a – , seelvoo-**play**?*
How do I get to – , please?

1. Excusez-moi, où est la rue de –?

3. C'est la bonne direction pour –?

2. Traversez la rue et prenez la première à droite.

5. C'est loin?

4. Suivez la direction de – .

1. *Exkuwzay-**mwa**, **oo**-ay la ruw duh –?*
   Excuse me, where is – street?
2. *Tra-**vair**say la ruw ay prunnay la prumyair a dr**watt**.*
   Cross the road and take the first right.
3. *Say la bon dee-**reks**yong poor –?*
   Is this the way to –?
4. *Sweevay la dee-**reks**yong duh – .*
   Take the road to – .
5. *Say lwang?*
   Is it far?

Directions/locations

les Toilettes
*lay twa-**let***
the Lavatory

Hommes/Messieurs
Gentlemen
Dames/Femmes
Ladies

Hors service
Out of order

Libre   *Occupé*
Vacant   Engaged

Tout Droit
too drwa
Straight On

à Gauche
a goshe
to the Left

to the Right
a drwatt
à Droite

au Coin
oh kwang
on the Corner

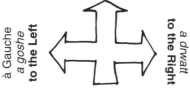

en Face de
on fass duh
Opposite

Derrière, Devant
*derry-**air**, duvvong*
Behind, in Front

le Carrefour
luh kaar-foor
the Crossroads

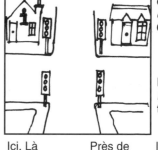

le Rond-point
luh rong pwang
the Roundabou

Jusqu'à
zhuw-ska
as Far as

Ici, Là
*ee-**see**, la*
Here, There

Près de
pray duh
Near to

les Feux
lay fur
the Traffic Ligh

> **Bon voyage!**
> *bong vwa-yazh*
> Have a good trip!

l'Auto/la Voiture
lohto/la vwa-tuwr
the Car

le Vélo, la Moto
luh vaylo, la moto
the Bicycle, Motorcycle

Je vais à pied
zhuvvay app-yay
I walk

Speed limits:
France: motorways* 130km (80mph), other roads* 110/90 (68/55), towns 50 (31)
Belgium: 120, 90, 50km (74, 55, 31mph)
Switzerland: 120, 80, 50km (74, 50, 31mph)   *10km less when wet

---

In town

Priorité à droite: traffic from the right has priority unless stated otherwise.

Toutes directions ▷
Through traffic

Bernay
Start of village & speed restriction

~~**Bernay**~~
End of village & speed restriction

CENTRE VILLE

AUTRES DIRECTIONS ⬆

Centre ville Town centre
Autres directions
'All other destinations', ie not already indicated

◁ **Sens Unique**
One-way street

Circulation/ Sens interdite
No entry

VEHICULES LENTS SERREZ À DROITE
Slow vehicles keep to right-hand lane

Déviation ▷
Diversion

Poids Lourds ▷
Heavy/long vehicles

AXE ROUGE
No stopping/Clearway

Sauf Riverains
Except for access

Expressway/motorway – *l'autoroute* – *lohto-root*

Péage – pay-aazh – toll   *Monnaie –* cash lane

Sortie
Exit

Aire de –
Lay-by/service area

un parking – a car park

un distributeur/un parcmètre – a ticket machine

Buy a card *(une carte de parcmètre)* from the *Tabac* (tobacconist).

Stationnement interdit

Défense de stationner

No parking

Fin d'interdiction de stationner

End of parking restrictions

2 heures maximum
Durée maximale 2h
Durée limitée à 2h

Maximum period 2 hrs

Non payant
limité a 2h

Free parking.
Limit 2 hrs
(usually for
disabled)

Stationnement
Payant   Gratuit

Parking
Paying   Free

Tous les jours

Every day

Paiement par pièces

Pay by cash

ou par carte

or by card

Sauf samedi, dimanche

Except Saturday, Sunday

Jours fériés, mois d'août

Public holidays, August

de 9h à 18h30

from 9.00 to 18.30

Meters

1 *Introduire votre Carte*	Insert card
2 *Choisir la DUREE*	Select PERIOD
3 *Validation/VALIDER votre Choix*	CONFIRM period required
4 *Retirer votre Carte*	Remove card
5 *Sortie du Ticket*	Take ticket here

ANNULER/Annulation	Press to CANCEL
Appuyez sur le Bouton	Press button
Pour CHANGER de Carte	Press to CHANGE card
1 pression = 1/4 d'heure	1 press = 15 mins.

Your	right	of	**Passage protégé** way	Danger	**Chaussée déformée** Subsidence	**Gravillons** Loose chippings

No longer your right of way

| **Cédez le passage** Give way | **Vous n'avez pas la priorité** Priority to traffic on roundabout | **Risque de verglas** Icy road | Fire risk **No** fires, matches, cigarettes etc. | **BREST Itinéraire bis** Holiday route avoiding traffic jams |

| **Ralentir** Slow down | **Rappel** Reminder | **Route barrée** Road closed |

Breakdown/emergencies (see also pp.51, 79; Repairs pp.68-70)

Look for orange emergency phones *Secours Routier* (free) or phone sign marked *Gendarmerie* – Police. *Pompiers* – Fire Brigade.

1. Je suis en panne.
2. Pouvez-vous m'aider, s'il vous plaît?
3. Puis-je utiliser votre téléphone?
4. Où est le garage le plus proche?
5. Quelle est la marque?
6. Où se trouve la voiture maintenant?

Instructions

State:

1. number of phone
2. location of accident (distance from phone, direction of traffic)
3. No. and type of vehicles involved
4. No. and condition of injured

*Zhuh sweezon **pan**.*
  I've broken down.

*Poovay-voo **medd**ay, seelvoo-**play**?*
  Can you help me, please?

*Pweezh uwtee-**lee**zay votr taylay-**fonn**?*
  May I use your phone?

4. ***Oo**-ay luh ga-**razh** luh pluw **prosh**?*
  Where is the nearest garage?

5. *Kellay la **maark**?*
  What make is it?

6. ***Oo** suh troov la vwa-**tuwr** mant-nong?*
  Where is the car now?

Le – ne marche pas.
Luh – nuh maarsh pa.
The – isn't working.

Elle ne démarre pas.
*Ell nuh day-**maar** pa.*
It won't start.

J'ai besoin d'un – .
Zhay buzzwang duhn
I need a – .

Le moteur cale/chauffe.
*Luh mott-**ur** kal/shoaf.*
The engine is stalling/overheating.

1. le Filtre à Air
   *luh feeltra **air***
   the Air Filter

2. la Batterie
   *la batter-**ree***
   the Battery

3. les Freins
   lay frang
   the Brakes

4. les Patins de Frein
   lay pattang duh frang
   the Brake Blocks

5. une Ampoule
   *uwn om-**pool***
   a Bulb

6. le Câble
   luh kaabl
   the Cable

7. le Carburateur
   *luh karbuwra-**tur***
   the Carburettor

8. la Chaîne
   la shen
   the Chain

9. le Starter
   *luh star-**tair***
   the Choke

10. l'Embrayage
    *lonbr-eye-**azh***
    the Clutch

11. l'Allumeur
    *lalluw-**mur***
    the Distributor

12. le Système Électrique
    *see-**stem** aylek**treek***
    the Electrical System

13. le Moteur
    *luh mott-**ur***
    the Engine

14. l'Échappement
    *lay-**shapp**mong*
    the Exhaust

15. la Courroie de Ventilateur
    *koor-wa duh vonteelat-**tur***
    the Fan Belt

16. un Fusible
    *uhn fuw-**zeebl***
    a Fuse

17. un Joint
    uhn zhwang
    a Gasket

18. les Vitesses
    *lay vee-**tess***
    the Gears

19. la Boîte de Vitesses
    *la bwatt duh vee-**tess***
    the Gearbox

20. le Guidon
    luh gheedong
    the Handlebars

1. le Phare
   luh faar
   the Headlight

2. une Chambre à Air
   *uwn shombra **air***
   an Inner Tube

3. la Clé
   la klay
   the Key

4. une Fuite (d'Huile/d'Eau)
   uwn fweet (dwee/(doh)
   an (Oil/Water) Leak

5. une Lampe
   uwn lomp
   a Light

6. le Porte-Bagages
   *luh port bag-**gazh***
   the Luggage Carrier

7. un Sandow (une Sangle)
   uhn sondo (uwn songl)
   a Luggage Elastic (Strap)

8. un Pare-Boue
   *uhn paar **boo***
   a Mudguard

9. un Écrou
   *uhn ay-**kroo***
   a Nut

10. une Sacoche
    *uwn sakk-**osh***
    a Pannier

11. les Vis Platinées
    *lay **veece** platty-nay*
    the Points

12. la Pompe
    la pomp
    the Pump

13. une Réparation Vélo
    *raypa-**rass**yong vaylo*
    a Puncture Kit

14. le Radiateur
    *luh raddya-**tur***
    the Radiator

35. une Vis
    uwn veece
    a Screw

36. un Tournevis
    uhn tournuh-veece
    a Screwdriver

37. un Amortisseur
    *uhn ammortee-**sur***
    a Shock Absorber

38. le Pot d'Échappement
    *poh day-**shapp**mong*
    the Silencer

39. une Clef (à Écrous)
    *uwn klay (a ay-**kroo**)*
    a Spanner

40. une Bougie
    *uwn boo-**zhee***
    a Sparking Plug

Location de Vélos
Cycle hire

41. des Rayons
    day rayong
    the Spokes

42. un Pneu
    *uhn p(uh)**nur***
    a Tyre

43. la Pression des Pneus
    *pressyong day p-**nur***
    the Tyre Pressure

44. une Valve
    uwn valve
    a Valve

45. une Roue
    uwn roo
    a Wheel

46. le Pare-brise
    luh pàar breeze
    Windscreen/-shield

47. les Essuie-glace
    *layzess-**wee** glass*
    the Wipers

des Chaînes de Neige
day shen duh nezh
some Snow Chains

j'ai crevé
zhay kruvvay
I've got a Puncture/Flat

Où est la station service la plus proche?
*Oo-ay la stassyong sair-**veece** la pluw **prosh**?*
Where is the nearest petrol station?

Libre-service	l'Essence
Self-service	*lessonce*
	Petrol/Gas
le Diesel/ Gazole	le GPL
*diesel/gazz-**oll***	*zhay pay **ell***
Diesel	LPG

l'Air	l'Huile	l'Eau
lair	*l-**weel***	*loh*
Air	Oil	Water

1. Le plein (du gazole), s'il vous plaît.

2. Pouvez-vous vérifier (l'huile/la pression des pneus), s'il vous plaît?

1. *Luh **plang** (duw gazz-**oll**), seelvoo-**play**.*
   Fill it up (with diesel), please.

2. *Poovay-voo **vay**reef-yay (l-weel/la pressyong day **pnur**), seelvoo-**play**?*
   Can you check (the oil/the tyre pressure), please?

Repairs

1. Qu'est-ce qui ne va pas?

2. Le – ne marche pas.

3. Pourriez-vous le réparer?

4. Combien de temps faut-il compter?

5. Combien vous dois-je

6. Merci beaucoup.

1. *Keskee nuh vappa?*
   What's the matter?

2. *Luh – nuh maarsh pa.*
   The – isn't working.

3. *Poory-ay voo luh ray-**parr**ay?*
   Can you repair it?

4. *Komb-yang duh tom foh-teel **kong**ta*
   How long will it take?

5. *Komb-yang voo dwazh?*
   What do I owe you?

6. *Mair-**see** boh-**koo**.*
   Thank you very much.

régler – to adjust   *tordu* – bent   *coincé* – st

a. *Bong-zhoor (mus-**yuh**/ma-**dam**). Zhay **ray**zairvay uwn vwa-**tuwr**, oh nom duh – .*
   Hello (sir/madam). I have booked a car. My name is – .

b. *Bong-zhoor (mus-**yuh**/ma-**dam**). Zhuh voodray looay uwn vwa-**tuwr**.*
   Hello (sir/madam). I'd like to hire a car.

. *Kell zhonruh duh vwa-**tuwr** – puh-**teet**, mwa-**yen**, grond?*
   What sort of car – small, medium, large?

*Poor uhn zhoor, uwn suh-**men**?*
   For one day, a week?

*Lassuw-**ronce** (kom-**plet**) ay kom-**preez**?*
   Is (comprehensive) insurance
   included?

*Esskuh zhuh pur rahndr la vwa-**tuwr** a
Lee-ong?*
   Can I leave the car in Lyons?

*Vwa-**see** mong pair-**mee** duh kong-
dweer.*
   Here is my driving licence.

2. *Say komb-yang paar (zhoor/suh-**men**)?*
   How much is it per (day/week)?

4. *Avvek keelomay-**trazh** ee-**lee**meetay?*
   Is it unlimited mileage?

6. ***Kong** dwazh **ram**munay la vwa-**tuwr**?*
   When do I have to return the car by?

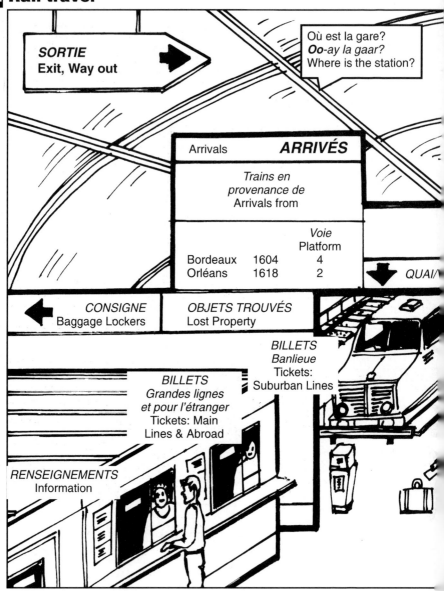

SORTIE
Exit, Way out

Où est la gare?
Oo-ay la gaar?
Where is the station?

Arrivals	**ARRIVÉS**	
Trains en provenance de Arrivals from		
		Voie Platform
Bordeaux	1604	4
Orléans	1618	2

QUAI/

CONSIGNE
Baggage Lockers

OBJETS TROUVÉS
Lost Property

BILLETS Banlieue
Tickets: Suburban Lines

BILLETS Grandes lignes et pour l'étranger
Tickets: Main Lines & Abroad

RENSEIGNEMENTS
Information

TIMETABLES
Autres trains – other trains
Circule/circulant ce jour-là – runs that day
 (ne...pas) – does not
Correspondance – connection
Dimanches et fêtes – Sundays & holidays
Hebdo/hebdomadaire – weekly
Jours ouvrables – weekdays

Jours particuliers – dates of possible changes
en Période de pointe – at peak period
Réservation obligatoire – booking obligatory
Sauf – except
Tous les jours – daily
Tous les 20 minutes – every 20 minut

un (le) train
uhn (luh) trang
a (the) Train

SNCF
French Railways

DÉPARTS — Departures

GRANDES LIGNES
Main Lines
BANLIEUE
Suburban Lines

Heure	Destination	Voie
Time	Destination	Platform
1710	Angoulème	5

◀ Platform

en tête/en queue
Front/Back of train

RESTAURATION ▶
SALLE d'ATTENTE ▶

Refreshments
Waiting Room

Timetable

HORAIRE

Date-stamping tickets
Pour valider votre billet compostez-le

On all transport you must punch your ticket (in orange machine at platform entrance).
Metro: punch tickets and passes
Buses: punch tickets only.

lundi – Monday
mardi à jeudi – Tues.-Thurs.
vendredi – Friday
samedi, dimanche – Sat., Sun.

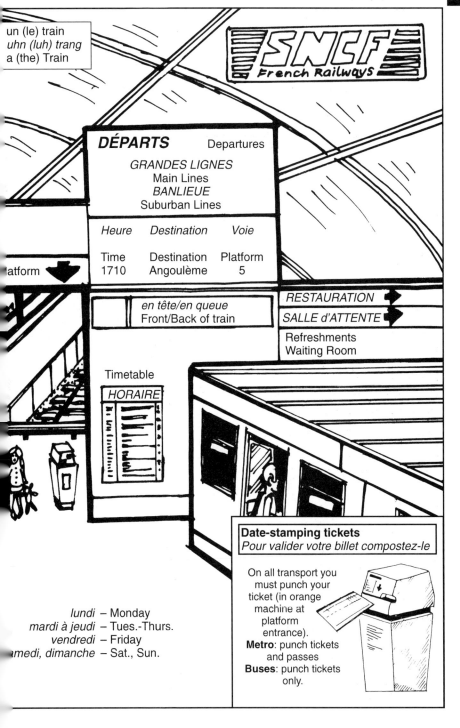

1. Un aller pour Toulouse, s'il vous plaît.
2. C'est combien?
3. Je voudrais réserver une (place/couchette).
4. A quelle heure part le train?

Où allez-vous?
Oo-allay voo?
Where are you going?

Je vais à – .
Zhuh vay a – .
I'm going to – .

un Aller Simple
a Single/One way

un Aller-retour
a Return/Round trip

Fumeur ou Non-fumeur
Smoker or Non-smoker

le Prochain/Dernier trair
proshang/**dairn**yay trai
the Next/Last train

1. *Uhn **al**-lay poor Too-**looz**, seelvoo-**play**.*
   A single to Toulouse, please.

2. *Say komb-yang?*
   How much is it?

3. *Zhuh voodray **ray**zairvay uwn (plass/koo-**shet**).*
   I'd like to book a (seat/couchette).

4. *A kell-**ur** paar luh **trang**?*
   When does the train go?

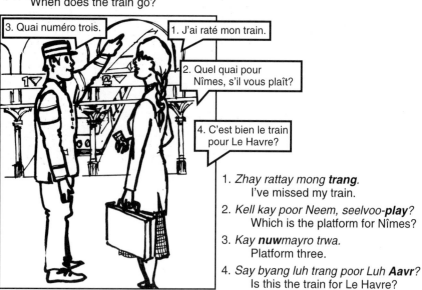

3. Quai numéro trois.
1. J'ai raté mon train.
2. Quel quai pour Nîmes, s'il vous plaît?
4. C'est bien le train pour Le Havre?

1. *Zhay rattay mong **trang**.*
   I've missed my train.

2. *Kell kay poor Neem, seelvoo-**play**?*
   Which is the platform for Nîmes?

3. *Kay **nuw**mayro trwa.*
   Platform three.

4. *Say byang luh trang poor Luh **Aavr**?*
   Is this the train for Le Havre?

Buses

un ticket	- a ticket
Entrée	- In
Sortie	- Out
Appuyez	- Press
Arrêt	- Stop
le Bus/l'autobus	- Local bus
le Car/l'autocar	- Coach
Correspondance	- Connection
la Gare routière	- Bus station
Vente de tickets	- Tickets sold here

1. Il y a des bus pour Versailles, s'il vous plaît?
2. Quand part le bus pour Montmartre?
3. D'où part le bus?
4. Quelle est la fréquence des bus?
5. Ça prend combien de temps?

1. *Eel-ya day buwss poor Vairs-eye, seelvoo-play?*
   Is there a bus to Versailles?

2. *Kong paar luh buwss poor Mong-maatr?*
   When does the bus for Montmartre go?

3. *Doo paar luh buwss?*
   Where does the bus go from?

4. *Kell-ay la fray-kahnss day buwss?*
   How often do the buses go?

5. *Sa pron komb-yang duh tom?*
   How long does it take?

Un carnet, s'il vous plaît.
Uhn karnay, seelvoo-play.
A book of ten tickets, please.

1. Est-ce que ce bus va à (la gare)?
2. Faut-il changer de bus?
3. C'est (la gare)?
4. Pouvez-vous me dire quand je dois descendre?

Tickets are sold on buses, at Tabacs or stations. Carnets (books of 10) are cheaper and may be used by several people. Tickets are usable on either bus or metro.

N.B. Remember to punch your ticket (p.73)

1. *Esskuh suh buwss va a (la gaar)?*
   Does this bus go to (the station)?

2. *Foh-teel shon-zhay duh buwss?*
   Do I have to change buses?

3. *Say (la gaar)?*
   Is this (the station)?

4. *Poovay-voo muh deer kong zhuh dwa des-sondr?*
   Can you tell me when to get off?

le Métro
luh maytro
Underground/subway (flat fare)

RER   Paris suburban network

Correspondance
Interchange

1. *Uhn teekay, seelvoo-**play**.*
   One ticket*, please.

2. *Pooray zhav-**waar** uhn plon
   duw maytro, seelvoo-**play**.*
   Could I have a plan of the
   metro, please.

3. *Kell **leen**yuh va alla toor
   Eff-**ell**?*
   Which line goes to the
   Eiffel Tower?

4. ***Foh**-teel shonzhay duh **trang***
   Do I have to change
   (trains)?

*see p. 75

Boats

1. D'où part le (bateau/ferry) pour Ajaccio?
2. Combien de temps dure la traversée?

3. Je voudrais réserver une
   (couchette/cabine).

1. *Doo paar luh (batto/fer-**ree**) poor A**zhaks**yo?*
   Where does the (boat/ferry) to Ajaccio go from?

2. *Komb-yang duh tom duwr la **trav**airsay?*
   How long is the crossing?

3. *Zhuh voodray **ray**zairvay
   uwn (koo-**shett**/ka-**been**).*
   I'd like to book a
   (berth/cabin).

Bâbord – Port
baabor

le Bateau, le Yacht
luh batto, luh yot
the Boat, Yacht

le Canal
luh canal
the Canal

une Ceinture
*uwn sang-**tuwr***
a Lifebelt

Tribord – Starboard
treebor

l'Écluse
*lay-**kluwz***
the Lock

le Port de Plaisance
por duh plezzonce
the Marina

le Moteur Hors-bord
*luh mott-**ur or** bor*
the Outboard Motor

un Gilet de Sauvetage
*uhn zheelay duh **sohv**-taazh*
a Life Jacket

le Quai
luh kay
the Quay

1. Où est le magasin d'accastillage?
2. Où puis-je me procurer (de l'eau/du gas-oil/des pains de glace)?
3. Où est la capitainerie du port?
4. Où puis-je trouver un mécanicien (de marine)?
5. Quand l'écluse (ouvre/ferme)-t-elle?

. **Oo**-ay luh magga-zang dakkasty-**azh**?
  Where is the chandlery?

. **Oo** pweezhuh muh **pro**kuwray (dull-**oh**/duw gazoil/day pang duh glass)?
  Where can I get (some water/some diesel/some blocks of ice)?

. **Oo**-ay la kappy-tenne**ree** duw por?
  Where is the harbour master's office?

. **Oo** pweezhuh troovay uhn mayka-**nees**yang (duh ma-**reen**)?
  Where will I find a (marine) engineer?

. **Kong** lay-**kluwz** (oovr/fairm) tell?
  When does the lock (open/close)?

l'Agent des Douanes
*lazhong day doo-**ann***
the Customs Officer

le Port d'Immatriculation
*luh **por** deema-trikuw-**las**yong*
the Port of Registry

Où puis-je avoir un bulletin météo?
Oo pweezhav-**waar** uhn buwl-tang **may**tayo?
Where can I get a weather forecast?

vis de Coup de Vent
vvy duh **koo** duh vong
ale Warning

aute/Basse Pression
at/bass pressyong
gh/Low Pressure

ent se renforçant/
ollissant/Modéré
ong suh rongforsong/
nollysong/moddayray
creasing/Decreasing/
oderate Wind

la Marée haute/basse
la marray oat/bass
High/Low Tide

la Mer
la mair
the Sea

Mer Agitée
mair azhy-tay
Rough Sea

Mer Calme
mair kal-m
Calm Sea

le Courant
luh koorong
the Tide/Current

Pour aller à l'aéroport, s'il vous plaît?
*Poor **al**-lay a la-**ay**ro-por, seelvoo-**play**?*
How do I get to the airport?

l'Avion
***lav**-yong*
the Plane

Porte   Arrivés (Départs)
Gate   Arrivals (Departures)

L'embarquement a lieu porte numéro – .
***lom**barkuh-mong a l-**yuh** port nuwmayro*
Boarding will take place at gate number – .

Dernier appel pour les passagers du vol – .
*dairn-yay ap-**pel** poor lay **pass**azhay duw **vo***
Last call for passengers on flight – .

1. ***Kong** paar luh proshang vol poor Zhuh-**nairv**?*
   When is the next flight to Geneva?

2. *A **nurv**-ur **deece**.*
   At 9.10.

4. *Kellay luh **nuw**mayro duw **vol**?*
   What is the flight number?

3. *A kell-**ur** ay lonruh-**zhees**truh-mong?*
   What time is check in?

5. *Set-uhn vol dee-**rekt**?*
   Is it a direct flight?

Problems, reservations

1. *Zhay rattay mong **av**-yong.*
   I've missed my plane.

2. *May bag-**gazh** nuh song pazza-**ree**vay.*
   My luggage hasn't arrived.

3. *Zhuh voodray (shonzhay/**ann**uwlay) ma rayzair-**vass**yong.*
   I'd like to (change/cancel) my reservation.

4. *Zhuh voodray uhn beeyay poor New York, luh **luhn**dee kattr (may), seelvoo-**play**.*
   I'd like a ticket to New York, for Monday 4 (May), please.

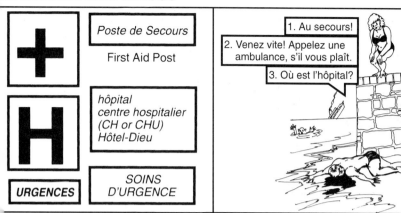

✚	Poste de Secours First Aid Post
H	hôpital centre hospitalier (CH or CHU) Hôtel-Dieu
URGENCES	SOINS D'URGENCE

1. Au secours!
2. Venez vite! Appelez une ambulance, s'il vous plaît.
3. Où est l'hôpital?

emergency services: Medical, ring 15 (SAMU) or see p.51
Minor ailments: *Pharmacie* p.44

. *Oh suh-**koor**!*
    Help!

. *Vunnay **veet!** **App**lay uwn ombuw-**lonce**, seelvoo-**play**.*
    Quick! Please call an ambulance.

*Oo-ay loppy-**tal**?*
    Where's the hospital?

Calling the doctor/making an appointment

1. S'il vous plaît, j'ai besoin (d'un docteur/d'une ambulance).
2. Je voudrais voir le docteur.
3. Quand puis-je venir? C'est urgent.

*Consultations
tous les jours
de 10h à 12h*
Surgery hours 10-12 daily

For emergency home visits ask Information (p.51) for *SOS Médecins*.

Though you must pay the doctor initially, with form E111 the French authorities will refund most later. (Note: E111 does not cover ambulance charges.)

*Seelvoo-**play**, zhay buzzwang (duhn dok-**tur**/duwn ombuw-**lonce**).*
    I need (a doctor/an ambulance).

*Zhuh voodray vwaar luh dok-**tur**.*
    I'd like to see the doctor.

*Kong pweezhuh vunn-**eer**? Set **uwr**-zhong.*
    When can I come? It's urgent.

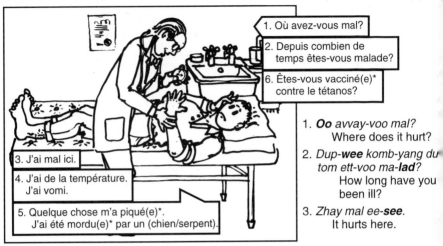

1. Où avez-vous mal?

2. Depuis combien de temps êtes-vous malade?

6. Êtes-vous vacciné(e)* contre le tétanos?

3. J'ai mal ici.

4. J'ai de la température. J'ai vomi.

5. Quelque chose m'a piqué(e)*. J'ai été mordu(e)* par un (chien/serpent).

1. *Oo avvay-voo mal?*
   Where does it hurt?

2. *Dup-**wee** komb-yang du tom ett-voo ma-**lad**?*
   How long have you been ill?

3. *Zhay mal ee-**see**.*
   It hurts here.

4. *Zhay dulla tompayra-**tuwr**. Zhay vom-**mee**.*
   I have a temperature. I've been sick.

5. *Kellkuh shoze ma **pee**kay. Zhay aytay mor-**duw** par uhn (shee-**ang**/sairpong).*
   I've been stung. I've been bitten by a (dog/snake).   *fem. adjective – p.94

6. *Ett-voo **vak**seenay kawntr luh **tay**tannoss?*
   Have you been vaccinated against tetanus?

1. Je prends ce médicament régulièrement.

2. Pouvez-vous me donner une ordonnance, s'il vous plaît?

3. Il ne faut rien manger.

4. Quel âge – avez-vous (a-t-il/elle)?

5. J'ai (Il/elle a) – ans.

6. Combien vous dois-je?

1. *Zhuh pron suh **may**deeka-mong rayguwl-**yair**mong.*
   I take this medicine regularly.

2. *Poovay-voo muh donnay uwn ordon-**nonce**, seelvoo-**play**?*
   Can you give me a prescription, please?

3. *Eel nuh **foh** ree-**ang** mongzhay.*
   You must not eat anything.

4. *Kell-**azh** – avvay-voo (a-**teel**/a-**tell**)?*
   How old – are you (is he/is she)?

5. *Zhay (Eel/ell a) – ong.*
   I am (He/she is) – years old.

6. *Komb-yang vous **dwazh**?*
   How much do I owe you?

une analyse de sang/d'urine
*uwn ana-leez duh song/duw-**reen***
a blood/urine sample

aking medicine:

. fois par jour
. times a day

outes les... heures
very... hours

vant/après les repas
efore/after meals

endant... jours
r... days

n cas de douleurs
 case of pain

u coucher
 bedtime

.6°F = 37°C

Essential information:

Je suis...   Zhuh swee...
I'm...   (sweez before a vowel)

allergique à (la pénicilline)
allair-**zheek** a (la payneesee-**leen**)
allergic to (penicillin)

asthmatique   diabétique
asma-**teek**   dee-abay**teek**
asthmatic   diabetic

épileptique   enceinte
aypeelep-**teek**   on-**sant**
epileptic   pregnant

Je fais de la tension
zhuh **fay** dulla tons-yong
I have high blood pressure

J'ai des ennuis cardiaques
zhay dayzon-**wee** kaardy-**akk**
I have heart trouble

---

t the dentist

hirurgien-Dentiste
rgences et Rendez-vous

mergencies and by appointment

1. J'ai mal au dents.

2. Puis-je prendre un rendez-vous (aussitôt que possible)?

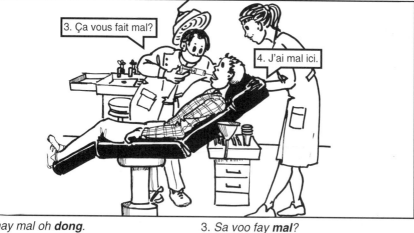

3. Ça vous fait mal?

4. J'ai mal ici.

Zhay mal oh **dong**.
  I've got toothache.

Pweezhuh prahndr uhn ronday-**voo**
(ohsee-**toh** kuh pos-**seebl**)?
  Can I make an appointment (as
  soon as possible)?

3. Sa voo fay **mal**?
  Does that hurt?

4. Zhay mal ee-**see**.
  It hurts here.

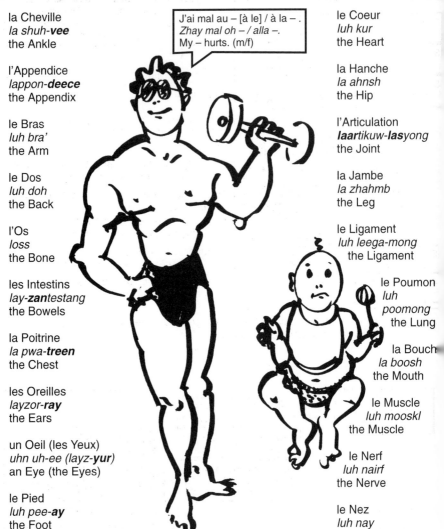

la Cheville
*la shuh-**vee***
the Ankle

l'Appendice
*lappon-**deece***
the Appendix

le Bras
luh bra'
the Arm

le Dos
luh doh
the Back

l'Os
loss
the Bone

les Intestins
*lay-**zan**testang*
the Bowels

la Poitrine
*la pwa-**treen***
the Chest

les Oreilles
*layzor-**ray***
the Ears

un Oeil (les Yeux)
*uhn uh-ee (layz-**yur**)*
an Eye (the Eyes)

le Pied
*luh pee-**ay***
the Foot

la Glande
la glahnd
the Gland

la Main
la mang
the Hand

la Tête
la tet
the Head

J'ai mal au – [à le] / à la – .
Zhay mal oh – / alla –.
My – hurts. (m/f)

le Coeur
luh kur
the Heart

la Hanche
la ahnsh
the Hip

l'Articulation
***laar**tikuw-**las**yong*
the Joint

la Jambe
la zhahmb
the Leg

le Ligament
luh leega-mong
the Ligament

le Poumon
*luh
poomong*
the Lung

la Bouche
la boosh
the Mouth

le Muscle
luh mooskl
the Muscle

le Nerf
luh nairf
the Nerve

le Nez
luh nay
the Nose

la Côte
la coat
the Rib

l'Épaule
*lay-**pole***
the Shoulder

l'Estomac
***lest**o-ma*
the Stomach

Sightseeing

1. Avez-vous des renseignements sur – ?

3. Quand le château ouvre-t-il?

5. Quelles promenades recommandez-vous dans les environs?

2. On peut visiter la vieille ville, le musée, le château...

4. C'est ouvert tous les jours sauf mardi.

Où se trouve l'Office de Tourisme?
*Oo suh troov loff-**eece** duh too-**reezm**?*
Where is the Tourist Office?

une Liste/des Brochures
*uwn leest/day bro-**shuwr***
a List/some Brochures

Many museums close Tuesdays or Mondays. Admission fees are often reduced on Sundays.

1. *Avvay-voo day ron-**sen**yuh-mong suwr*
   Have you any information about – ?

2. *Ong pur **vee**zeetay la vee-**ay** veel, luh muwzay, luh shatto.*
   You can visit the old town, the museum, the chateau...

3. *Kong luh shatto oovr-teel?*
   When is the chateau open?

4. *Set oo-**vair** too lay zhoor soaf maardee.*
   It's open every day except Tuesday

. *Kell prommuh-**nad** rukkuh-**monn**day voo dong layzon-**veer**ong?*
   Can you recommend any walks round here?

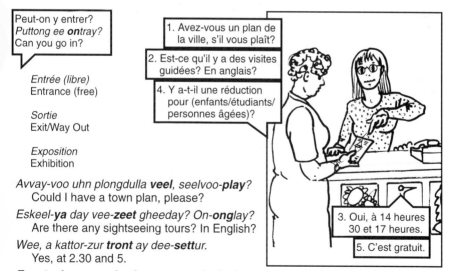

Peut-on y entrer?
*Puttong ee **on**tray?*
Can you go in?

Entrée (libre)
Entrance (free)

Sortie
Exit/Way Out

Exposition
Exhibition

1. Avez-vous un plan de la ville, s'il vous plaît?

2. Est-ce qu'il y a des visites guidées? En anglais?

4. Y a-t-il une réduction pour (enfants/étudiants/ personnes âgées)?

3. Oui, à 14 heures 30 et 17 heures.

5. C'est gratuit.

*Avvay-voo uhn plongdulla **veel**, seelvoo-**play**?*
Could I have a town plan, please?

*Eskeel-**ya** day vee-**zeet** gheeday? On-**ong**lay?*
Are there any sightseeing tours? In English?

*Wee, a kattor-zur **tront** ay dee-**sett**ur.*
Yes, at 2.30 and 5.

*Ee a-**teel** uwn ray-**duwks**yong poor (onfon/ay-**tuwd**yong/pair-**sonn** azhay)?*
Are there reductions for (children/students/pensioners)?

*Say grat-**wee**.*
It's free.

Booking entertainment p.86

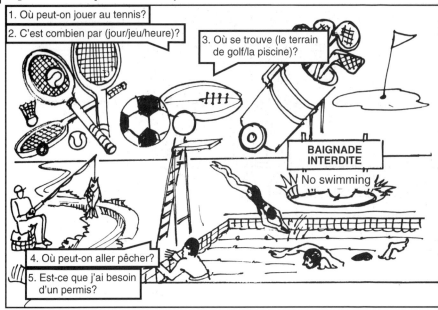

1. Où peut-on jouer au tennis?
2. C'est combien par (jour/jeu/heure)?
3. Où se trouve (le terrain de golf/la piscine)?
4. Où peut-on aller pêcher?
5. Est-ce que j'ai besoin d'un permis?

BAIGNADE INTERDITE

No swimming

1. *Oo puttong zhoo-ay oh tunny?*
   Where can you play tennis?

2. *Say **komb**-yang paar (zhoor/zhur/ur)?*
   How much is it per (day/game/hour)?

3. *Oo suh troov (luh **terr**ang duh golf/la pee-**seen**)?*
   Where is (the golf course/the swimming pool)?

4. *Oo purtong allay peshay?*
   Where can you go fishing?

5. *Esskuh zhay buzzwang duhn pair-**mee**?*
   Do I need a permit?

1. Est-ce que je peux louer... *Esskuh zhuh pur **loo**-ay* Can I hire...	2. Où peut-on faire... *Oo puttong fair* Where can you go...

une Raquette de Tennis (des Balles)
*uwn rack-**ett** duh tunny (day **bal**)*
a Tennis Racket (some Balls)

des Clubs de Golf
day club duh golf
some Golf Clubs

une Planche à Voile
*uwn plonsh a **vwal***
a Surfboard

du Cheval
*duw shuh-**val***
Riding

du Bateau
duw batto
Sailing

du Surf
duw surf
Surfing

du Ski Nautique
*duw skee noh-**teek***
Water Skiing

de la Planche à Vo...
*dulla plonsh a **vwa**...*
Windsurfing

Location de Skis
Ski Hire

3. Quelle pointure faites-vous?

1. Puis-je prendre des leçons de ski?
2. Je voudrais louer – .
4. C'est combien le forfait?

le Remonte-Pente
*luh ruh-**mawnt pahnt***
the Ski Tow

des Patins à Glace
*day pattang a **glass***
some Skates

une Luge
uwn luwzh
a Sledge

un Snowboard
uhn snowboard
a Snowboard

. *Pweezhuh prahndr day lussong duh **skee**?*
Can I have some skiing lessons?

. *Zhuh voodray loo-ay*
I'd like to hire – .

3. *Kell pwan-**tuwr** fett voo?*
What's your shoe size?

4. *Say **komb**-yang luh forfay?*
How much is a lift pass?

des Skis Alpins
*day skee oll-**pang***
some Downhill Skis

les Fixations
*lay feek-**sas**yong*
Bindings

des Bâtons
day battong
some Ski Sticks

des Skis de Fond
*day skee duh **fong***
Cross-country Skis

des Chaussures de Ski
*shoh-**suwr** duh skee*
some Ski Boots

le Téléphérique
*luh taylayfay-**reek***
the Cable Car

On the piste

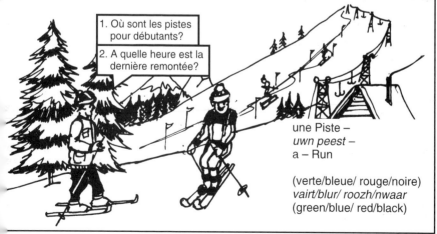

1. Où sont les pistes pour débutants?
2. A quelle heure est la dernière remontée?

une Piste –
uwn peest –
a – Run

(verte/bleue/ rouge/noire)
vairt/blur/ roozh/nwaar
(green/blue/ red/black)

*Oo song lay peest poor **day**-buwtong?*
Where are the beginners' runs?

2. *A kell-**ur** ayla dairn-yair ru**mawn**tay?*
What time is the last ascent?

1. Qu'est-ce qu'on joue au (cinéma/théâtre) ce soir?

2. Je voudrais deux billets pour samedi (après-midi/soir).

3. Quand est-ce que ça commence/finit?

4. A quel prix?

5. – francs, environ.

1. *Kesskong zhoo oh (**see**-nayma/tay-**aatr**) suh swaar?*
   What's on at the (cinema/theatre) this evening?

2. *Zhuh voodray dur beeyay poor samdee (appray-**mee**dee/swaar).*
   I'd like two tickets for <u>Saturday</u> (afternoon/evening).

3. *Kong esskuh sa kom-monce/fee-nee?*
   When does it start/finish?

4. *A kell **pree**?*
   What price?

5. *– frong, ong-**veer**ong.*
   About – francs.

1. Est-ce qu'il y a (une discothèque) par ici?

2. Je voudrais aller...

1. *Eskeel-**ya** (uwn deesko-**tek**) paar ee-**see**?*
   Is there (a disco) here?

2. *Zhuh voodray **al**-lay*
   I'd like to go...

au Concert	à un Match de Football	demain
*oh kon-**sair***	*a uhn match duh **foot** ba-l*	*duh-**mang***
to a Concert	to a Football Match	tomorrow
à un Concert Pop	ce soir	vendredi
*a uhn kon-sair **pop***	*suh swaar*	*vondruhdee*
to a Pop Concert	tonight	on Friday*

*days p.

1. Bonjour. Comment allez-vous?
2. Très bien – et vous?
3. Je m'appelle – . Comment vous appelez-vous?
4. Voici... mon mari (ma femme), mon fils (ma fille), mon ami(e).
5. Enchanté.
6. Au revoir.

*Bong-zhoor. Kommon **tal**-lay voo?*
Hello. How are you?

Tray byang – ay voo?
Fine, thanks – and you?

*Zhumma-**pell** – . Kommon voo-**zapp**lay voo?*
My name is – . What's yours?

4. *Vwa-**see**... mong marry (ma fam), mong feece (ma fee), monna-**mee**.*
This is... my husband (my wife), my son (my daughter), my friend [m/f].

5. *On-**shon**tay.*
Pleased to meet you.

6. *Oh ruv-**waar**.*
Goodbye.

1. Salut! Je m'appelle – .
2. Voici (mon frère/ma soeur).
3. As-tu des frères et des soeurs?
4. Quel âge as-tu?
5. J'ai treize* ans.

*Sa-**luw**. Zhumma-**pell***
Hi! My name is – .

*Vwa-**see** (mong frair/ma sur).*
This is (my brother/my sister).

***A tuw** day frair ay day sur?*
Have you any brothers and sisters?

4. *Kell **azh** a **tuw**?*
How old are you?

5. *Zhay trezzong.*
I'm 13.*

*Numbers p.112

1. *Ay-suh la prumyair **fwa** kuh voo vunnay on Frahnce?*
   Is this your first visit to France?
2. *Wee (Nong.) Zhunnuh paarl pa b-yang fronsay.*
   Yes (No.) I don't speak French very well.
3. *Esskuh voo voo **plezz**ay ee-**see**?*
   Do you like it here?
4. *Wee, zhuh-**lem** boh-**koo**.*
   Yes, I like it very much.
5. ***Doo** ett voo?*
   Where do you come from?
6. *Zha-**beet** a Lawndr.*
   I live in London.
7. *Kuh **fet** voo?*
   What do you do?
8. *Zhuh swee... (aytuwdy-**ong** (-**ont**), ruh-**trett**ay).*
   I'm a... (student, pensioner).
   *fem. adjective – p.9
9. *Kom-byang duh **tom** restay voo?*
   How long are you staying?
10. *Zhuh paar sam-**dee**.*
   I'm leaving on Saturday.

Accepting an invitation

French has its own versions of

London – Londres – *Lawndr*
Edinburgh – Édimbourg – ***Ay**dang-boor*
Dover – Douvres – *Doovr*
Montreal – Montréal – *Mawngray-**al***
Quebec – Québec – *kay-bekk*

1. ***Ett**-voo leebr suh **swaar**?*
   Are you free this evening?
2. *Voolay-voo (prahndr uhn **vair**)?*
   Would you like (to come for a drink)?
3. *Voll-**onty**-ay. Mair-**see** boh-**koo**.*
   That would be nice. Thank you ve much.
4. ***Kong** noo ruh-**troo**vong noo? **Oo**?*
   When shall we meet? Where?

1. Bonjour. (Bonsoir.)
2. Asseyez-vous, je vous en prie.
3. Qu'est-ce que vous prenez? (un café, du vin, une boisson non-alcoolisée)
4. Servez-vous. Encore un petit peu?
5. Oui, merci. (Non, merci.)
6. Ça vous plaît?
7. C'est délicieux!
8. Aimez-vous les sports, la lecture, danser, la musique?
9. J'aime bien –.

. *Bong-zhoor. (Bong-swaar.)*
  Hello. (Good evening.)

. ***Assay**ay-voo, zhuh voozon-**pree**.*
  Please sit down.

. *Kesskuh voo prunnay? (uhn kaff-**ay**, duw vang, uwn bwassong nong alko-olly-zay)*
  What would you like to drink? (a coffee, some wine, a soft drink)

. *Sairvay-**voo**. Ong-**kor** uhn putty **pur**?*
  Please help yourself. A little more?

5. *Wee, mair-**see**. (Nong, mair-**see**.)*
  Yes, please. (No, thanks.)

6. *Sa voo **play**?*
  Do you like it?

7. *Say dayleece-**yur**!*
  It's delicious!

8. ***Emm**ay-voo lay spor, la lek-**tuwr**, donsay, la muw-**zeek**?*
  Do you like sport, reading, dancing, music?

9. *Zhem byang – .*
  I like – .

Saying goodbye

2. Au revoir – et à bientôt!
1. Merci pour tout. (J'ai) passé un agréable moment. (Nous avons...)

*Mair-**see** poor **too**. (Zhay) passay uhn agray-**aabl** mohmong. (Noo-**zavv**ong)*
  Thanks for everything. (I've) had a lovely time. (We've...)

*Oh ruv-**waar** – ay ab-**yan**to!*
  Goodbye – and see you soon!

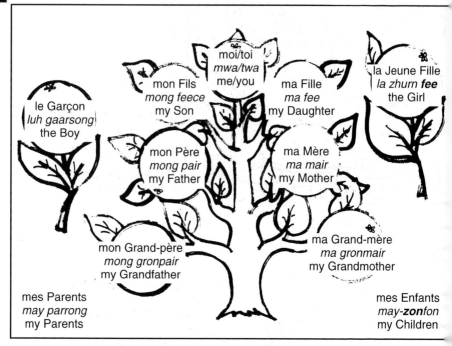

mon Fils
mong feece
my Son

moi/toi
mwa/twa
me/you

ma Fille
ma fee
my Daughter

la Jeune Fille
*la zhurn **fee***
the Girl

le Garçon
luh gaarsong
the Boy

mon Père
mong pair
my Father

ma Mère
ma mair
my Mother

mon Grand-père
mong gronpair
my Grandfather

ma Grand-mère
ma gronmair
my Grandmother

mes Parents
may parrong
my Parents

mes Enfants
*may-**zon**fon*
my Children

Countries and nationalities

Je suis (français/française).
Zhuh swee (fronsay/fron-**sez**)*
I am – French [masc./fem.]

D'où êtes-vous?
***Doo** ett voo?*
Where are you from?

*sweez before a vowe

Je suis (belge/suisse/luxembourgeois/e).
Zhuh swee (belzh/sweess/luwxom-boorzhwa/z).
I'm (from Belgium/Switzerland/Luxembourg).

l'Angleterre	anglais/anglaise	l'Irlande	irlandais/irlandaise
*longluh-**tair***	*(z)**ong**lay/ong**lez***	*eer-**lahnd***	*(z)**eer**londay/-lon**dez***
England	English	Ireland	Irish
le Pays de Galles	gallois/galloise	l'Écosse	écossais/écossaise
*luh payee duh **gal***	*galwa/gal-**waz***	*lay-**koss***	*(z)**ay**kossay/-ko**ssez***
Wales	Welsh	Scotland	Scottish

l'Australie	le Canada	la Nouvelle-Zélande	les États-Unis
*lohstral-**lee***	*luh kanna-**da***	*la noo**vell** zay**lahnd***	*layzay tazuw-**nee***
Australia	Canada	New Zealand	the USA

l'Allemagne	l'Italie	l'Espagne
*lal-**man**yuh*	*leeta-**lee***	*less-**pan**yuh*
Germany	Italy	Spain

1. *Oh voll-**ur**!*
   Stop thief!
2. ***Al**-lay voo-**zong**!*
   Go away!
3. ***Less**ay-mwa trong-**keel**!*
   Leave me alone!

.. and problems

1. *Zhay pair-**duw** (mong passpor/may trav-**lair**).*
   I've lost (my passport/my traveller's cheques).
2. *Ong ma vollay (mong sack).*
   (My bag) has been stolen.
3. *Kommon **ay**-suh? Keskeel **yavv**ay duh-**dong**?*
   What does it look like? What was in it?
4. ***Oo** a-**beet**ay voo?*
   Where are you staying?
5. *Rom-**pless**ay suh formuw-**lair**, seelvoo-**play**.*
   Please fill in this form.

*Oo-ay luh posst duh poh-**leece**?*
   Where is the police station?

*Poovay-voo **medd**ay?*
   Can you help me?

*Zhay aytay a-**takk**ay.*
   I've been attacked.

*Zhuh **nayp**a daarzhong.*
   I have no money.

*Kuh poo-**ray** zhuh fair?*
   What should I do?

1. Où est le poste de police?
2. Pouvez-vous m'aider?
3. J'ai été attaqué.
4. Je n'ai pas d'argent.
5. Que pourrais-je faire?

...om	Prénom	Adresse	Quand	Où	}?
...ng	*praynong*	*a-**dress***	*kong*	*Oo*	
...urname	1st Name	Address	When	Where	

hier
*ee-**air***
Yesterday

aujourd'hui
*oh zhoord-**wee***
Today

demain
*duh-**mang***
Tomorrow

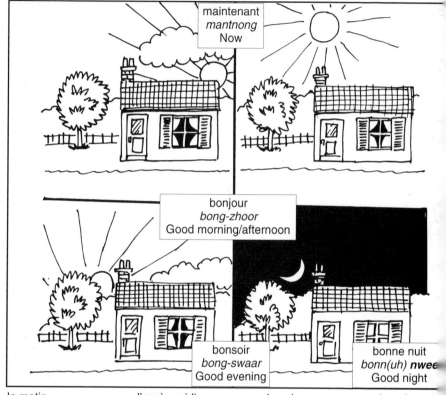

maintenant
mantnong
Now

bonjour
bong-zhoor
Good morning/afternoon

bonsoir
bong-swaar
Good evening

bonne nuit
*bonn(uh) **nwee***
Good night

le matin
luh mattang
(in) the morning

l'après-midi
*lappray-**mee**dee*
(in) the afternoon

le soir
luh swaar
(in) the evening

la nuit
la nwee
at (the) night

Days of the week – *la semaine* – *la suh-**men***

lundi
luhndee
Monday

mardi
maardee
Tuesday

mercredi
***mair**kruh-dee*
Wednesday

jeudi
zhurdee
Thursday

vendredi
***von**druh-dee*
Friday

samedi
samdee
Saturday

dimanche
deemonsh
Sunday

en hiver	onny-**vair**	in Winter

Joyeux Noël
*zh-wye-**ur** no-**el***
Merry
Christmas

Bonne Année
bon annay
Happy New Year

il neige
eel nezh
it's Snowing

décembre
day-sahmbr
DECEMBER

janvier
zhongvee-ay
JANUARY

février
fayvree-ay
FEBRUARY

au printemps	oh prantong	in Spring

Pâques
pakk
Easter

il pleut
eel plur
it's Raining

il fait du vent
*eel fay duw **vong***
it's Windy

mars
maarce
MARCH

avril
*av-**reel***
APRIL

mai
may
MAY

en été	on aytay	in Summer

j'ai chaud
*zhay **shoh***
I'm Hot

il fait chaud
*eel fay **shoh***
it's Hot

juin
zhwang
JUNE

juillet
zhwee-ay
JULY

août
oot
AUGUST

en automne	on oh-**tom**	in Autumn/Fall

la vendange
la von-donzh
the Wine Harvest

il fait froid
*eel fay **frwa***
it's Cold

septembre
septombr
SEPTEMBER

octobre
ok-tobbr
OCTOBER

j'ai froid
*zhay **frwa***
I'm Cold

novembre
*nov-**vomb**r*
NOVEMBER

Things: nouns In French all nouns are masculine (m) or feminine (f).

A: for one item only, ie **singular** (s), use *un* (m) or *une* (f):
un garçon a boy, *un billet* a ticket   *une fille* a girl, *une chambre* a room.

For more than one, ie **plural** (pl), use *des* for both genders: *des garçons* some boys
des billets some tickets, *des filles* some girls, *des chambres* some rooms.

Nouns usually add **s** in the plural, though it is not pronounced: *chambre/chambres*.
Some add **x** (also silent): *gâteau/gâteaux* * cake/s.
Animal, journal (animal, newspaper) change to *animaux*, journaux.*
Nouns ending in **-s, -x** or **-z** do not change.   (*aux* pronounced *oh*)

The: le for masculine nouns: *le billet* the ticket,
la for feminine ones: *la chambre* the room, **l'** before a vowel: *l'homme* the man.
In the plural use **les** for both genders: *les billets, les chambres, les hommes*.

Describing words: adjectives
If a noun is masculine, the adjective describing it will be too. If it is feminine or there
more than one, it usually adds **e** or **s**:

le livre vert the green book	*les livres verts* the green books
la carte verte the green card	*les cartes vertes* the green cards

Most adjectives follow the words they describe, apart from common ones such a
grand/grande (big), *petit/petite* (small), *premier/première* (first), *bon/bonne* (good).

It's mine: possessives
Unlike English, these depend on the gender of the item, not the owner,
eg *mon billet* my ticket, *ma voiture* my car, *mes fleurs* my flowers.

	m.	f.	pl.		m.	f.	pl.
my	*mon*	*ma*	*mes*	our	*notre*	*notre*	*nos*
*your s.	*ton*	*ta*	*tes*	*your pl.	*votre*	*votre*	*vos*
his, her, its	*son*	*sa*	*ses*	their	*leur*	*leur*	*leurs*

                                                    *see **you** under pronoun
There is no difference between his, her, its or their:
         son fils = his/her/its/their son   *sa maison* = his/her/its/their house
                 ses chambres = his/her/its/their rooms

I, you, it: pronouns These are shown with the verbs. The words for 'it' and 'they' diffe
depending on whether the noun is masculine or feminine:
la chambre est grande the room is big   *elle est grande* it is big

*__you (your):__ use *vous (votre)* whether talking to one person or several, since *tu* is f
children, close friends and family.

Action: verbs
Dictionaries show verbs in the infinitive, ie 'to' form. Endings change for each person.

to be	être	to have to	devoir
I am	je suis	I must	je dois
(you are	tu es)	(you must	tu dois)
he/she/it is	il/elle est	he/she/it must	il/elle doit
we are	nous sommes	we must	nous devons
you are	vous êtes	you must	vous devez
they are	il/elles sont	they must	ils doivent
I was/have been	j'ai été	I had to	j'ai dû

to have	avoir	to want	vouloir
I have	j'ai	I want	je veux
(you have	tu as)	(you want	tu veux)
he/she/it has	il/elle a	he/she/it wants	il/elle veut
we have	nous avons	we want	nous voulons
you have	vous avez	you want	vous voulez
they have	ils/elles ont	they want	ils/elles veulent
I had/have had	j'ai eu	I wanted to	j'ai voulu

to go	aller	to be able	pouvoir
I go	je vais	I can	je peux
you go	tu vas)	(you can	tu peux)
he/she/it goes	il/elle va	he/she/it can	il/elle peut
we go	nous allons	we can	nous pouvons
you go	vous allez	you can	vous pouvez
they go	ils/elles vont	they can	ils/elles peuvent
I went/have been	je suis allé (allée – f)	I was able to	j'ai pu

Many common or 'regular' verbs end in -er, eg **parler** – **to speak**:

je parle	nous parlons	il/elle parle	ils/elles parlent
(tu parles)	vous parlez	I spoke/have spoken	j'ai parlé

Saying no
Put ne in front of the verb and pas after it: je ne parle pas français
I don't speak French; je n'ai pas d'argent I haven't any money.

Questions
Take a statement, eg Vous parlez anglais You speak English, and
1. say it as if it were a question, with your voice rising at the end;
2. turn the verb round: Parlez-vous anglais? Do you speak English?
3. put est-ce que in front: Est-ce que vous parlez anglais? Do you speak English?

nouns	*m* masculine	*f* feminine	*pl* plural	Most adjectives have
the	le	la	les	feminine endings (see
a (some)	un	une	des	p.94), shown here as /e.

French-English

See also **Menu guide** pp. 30-35, **meat** p. 38, **fish** p. 39, **fruit & vegetables** pp. 40–41, the **body** 82, **car parts** p. 68, **colours** front cover, **days** p. 92, **numbers** p. 112. fc/bc front/back cover

A

à to; **au/à la, aux** to the (*s/pl*)
accueil (le bureau d') reception
acheter to buy
l' **addition** *f* bill, check
l' **aéroport** *m* airport
aider to help
l' **alimentation** *f* food shop
aller to go; l'**~-retour** *m* return ticket; l'**~-simple** *m* single ticket
l' **antigel** *m* antifreeze
août August
l' **appel** *m* call; **appeler** to call
l' **appendice** *m* appendix
l' **appétit** *m* appetite; **bon ~** enjoy your meal
après after; l'**après-midi** *m/f* afternoon
l' **arrêt** *m* stop
l' **articulation** *f* the joint
l' **ascenseur** *m* lift
assez enough, fairly
l' **assurance** *f* insurance
attendre to wait
attention! take care!
aujourd'hui today
l' **autoroute** *f* motorway
autre other
avant before
avec with
l' **avion** *m* plane
avoir to have; **~ besoin de** to need
avril April

B

le **bac** ferry
le **bain** bath
le **ball-trap** clay-pigeon shooting
le **bateau** boat
la **batterie** battery
beau/belle beautiful
beaucoup (de) many, much, a lot (of)
bien good, well; **~ sûr** of course
le **billet** ticket
blanc/blanche white
bleu/bleue blue
boire to drink
le **bois** wood, forest

la **boisson** drink
la **boîte** tin/can, box; night club; **~ de vitesses** gearbox
bon/ne good
bonjour hello; **bonsoir** good evening
la **bouche** mouth
la **bougie** sparking plug; candle
la **bouteille** bottle
le **bras** arm
le **brouillard** fog
brûlé/e burnt
brun/e brown
le **bureau** office

C

ça that; **ça va** OK
le **cadeau** gift
la **caisse** cash desk
la **campagne** country, - side
le **car** coach
le **carrefour** crossroads
la **carte** map, card, menu; **~ postale** postcard
cassé/e broken
la **caution** deposit
cédez le passage give way
le **centre - commercial** shopping centre; **~-ville** town centre
c'est it is
la **chaise** chair
la **chambre** bedroom; **~ d'hôte** B&B
le **château** castle
chaussée déformée road subsidence
le **chemin** path
la **cheminée** chimney, fire
cher/chère dear, expensive
le **cheval** horse
la **chose** thing
la **clé** key
la **climatisation** air-conditioning
le **coin** corner
le **collant** tights
combien how much/many
comme as, like
comment how
le **commissariat** police station
complet full; wholemeal (bread)
composer to dial

composter to validate a ticket
comprendre to understand;
  compris/e included; understood
le **compteur** meter
conduire to drive
continuer to continue
contre against
la **côte** coast; rib
la **couverture** blanket
la **crème** cream
la **croisière** cruise
le **cuir** leather

D

d'accord OK, all right
dans in
de of; **du/de la, des** of the (*s/pl*)
décembre December
défense de... no... ; ~ fumer no
  smoking; **~ d'entrer** no admittance
la **dégustation** wine/food tasting
le **déjeuner** lunch; **le petit déjeuner**
  breakfast
demain tomorrow
sur demande on request; **demander** to ask
  for
le/la **demi/e** half
la **dent** tooth; **la dentelle** lace
le **dépannage** breakdown service
le **départ** departure
depuis since
déranger to disturb
dernier/dernière last
derrière behind
descendre to get off
désolé/e sorry
devant in front of
dimanche Sunday
le **dîner** dinner
la **douane** customs
la **douche** shower
le **drap** sheet
à droite to the right
dur/e hard

E

l' **eau** *f* water
l' **école** *f* school
écrire to write; **par écrit** in writing
l' **église** *f* church
l' **électricité** *f* electricity
l' **emplacement** *m* pitch
emporter to take away
enchanté/e pleased to meet you
encore again, still
l' **enfant** *m/f* child
entier/entière whole
l' **entrée** *f* entrance; **entrez!** come in!

environ approximately
envoyer to send
l' **épaule** *f* shoulder
l' **épicerie** *f* grocer's
l' **équitation** *f* horse riding
l' **erreur** *f* mistake
l' **escalier** *m* stairs
essayer to try
l' **essence** *f* petrol/gas
est is; **l'est** *m* east
l' **étage** *m* floor, storey
l' **été** *m* summer
l' **étudiant/e** *m/f* student
l' **exposition** *f* exhibition

F

en **face** opposite
faire to do, make
la **fenêtre** window
le **fer** iron
la **ferme** farm
fermer to close
la **fête** festival, celebration
les **feux** traffic lights
février February
la **fille** girl, daughter
le **filtre** filter
finir to finish
la **fin** end
la **fleur** flower
le **foie** liver
la **foire** show, exhibition
la **fois** time; **une ~** once; **deux ~** twice
le **foot(ball)** football
la **forêt** forest, wood
fort/e strong
frais/fraiche fresh, cool
fumer to smoke

G

gardé/e guarded
la **gare** station
se **garer** to park
le **gâteau** cake
à gauche to the left
gazeux/-euse fizzy
le **genou** knee
gentil/le kind
le **glaçon** ice cube
la **glande** gland
la **gorge** throat
goûter to taste
grand/e big, tall
gratuit/e free
les **gravillons** *mpl* loose chippings
gris/e grey
gros/se big
le **guichet** ticket office

le **guide** guide, ~ book

H

la **hanche** the hip
haut/e high
hebdo,-madaire weekly
l' **heure** f hour, time
hier yesterday
l' **hiver** m winter
l' **homme** m man
l' **hôpital** m hospital
l' **horaire** m timetable
hors (de) ~ out of; ~ **saison** out of
season; ~ **service** out of order
l' **hôtel** m **de ville** town hall

I

ici here
il faut it is necessary
il y a there is/are
l' **île** f island
l' **immatriculation** f registration
inclus/e included
l' **infusion** f herbal tea
interdit/e prohibited
les **intestins** mpl bowels

J

j'ai (avoir) I have
jamais never
janvier January
le **jardin** garden, park
jaune yellow
jeune young
le **jeu/x** game/s
jeudi Thursday
joli/e pretty
le **jour** day; ~ **férié** holiday
le **journal** newspaper
juillet July
juin June
le **jus** juice; gravy
jusqu'à up to, until

L

là there; **là-bas** over there
le **lac** lake
la **laine** wool
le **lait** milk
la **langue** tongue
le **lavabo** washbasin
lent/e slow; **lentement** slowly
la **lessive** soap powder
la **librairie** bookshop, newsagent
libre unoccupied; ~-**service** self-service
le **ligament** ligament
la **ligne** line
le **linge** clothing/washing

le **lit** bed
le **livre** book
location de hire of
loin far
les **loisirs** mpl leisure
longtemps a long time
à louer for hire
lourd/e heavy
la **lumière** light
lundi Monday
les **lunettes** fpl glasses

M

le **magasin** shop
mai May
la **main** hand
mais but
la **maison** house; home-made
mal badly; ~ **de** – pain in –
malheureusement unfortunately
le **marché** market
marcher to walk/function
mardi Tuesday
la **marée** tide
le **mari** husband; **marié/e** married
marron brown
mars March
mauvais/e bad
le **médecin** doctor
le **médicament** medicine
même same; even
ménager/ménagère household
le **menu** set menu
la **mer** sea
merci thank you
mercredi Wednesday
la **mère** mother
mettre to put
midi midday; **le Midi** south of France
moi me
moins less; to (time)
le **mois** month
la **moitié** half
le **morceau** piece
le **musée** museum

N

n'est-ce pas? isn't it?
nager to swim
la **neige** snow
neuf/neuve new
ni... ni neither
Noël Christmas
noir/e black
le **nom** name
non no, not; ~ **compris** excluded
la **note** bill, check
nouveau/nouvelle new

novembre November
la **nuit** night; **nuitée** overnight stay
le **numéro** number

O

obtenir to obtain
occupé/e taken, occupied
l' **oeil** *m* eye
octobre October
l' **office** *m* **de tourisme** tourist office
à l' **ombrage** in the shade
orange orange
l' **ordonnance** *f* prescription
l' **oreille** *f* ear
l' **orteil** *m* toe
ou or
où where
l' **ouest** *m* west
oui yes
ouvert/e open; **ouvrir** to open

P

le **pain** bread, loaf
la **panne** breakdown
le **pantalon** trousers
Pâques Easter
la **papeterie** stationer's
le **papier** paper
le **paquet** packet
par by, per
le **parc** park
à **partir de** from
le **parfum** perfume; flavour
parler to speak
partir to leave
ne..pas not
payer to pay
le **péage** toll
la **pêche** peach; fishing
le **permis** licence
la **personne** person; **ne...** no one
pepit/e small
peu little (amount)
la **pharmacie** pharmacy
le **pied** foot
les **piétons** *mpl* pedestrians
la **pile** battery
la **piscine** swimming pool
la **piste** track, ski run
la **place** (town) square
la **plage** beach
plein/e full; **en plein air** outside
plus more; **ne... plus** no more/longer
le **pneu** tyre
le **poids** weight; ~ **lourd** heavy goods vehicle
la **pointure** shoe size
le **pont** bridge

le **port** harbour
la **porte** door
la **poste de secours** first aid post
le **poumon** lung
pour for
prendre to take
près (de) near (to)
présenter to introduce
le **préservatif** condom
pressé/e in a hurry; squeezed
la **pression** draught
prêt/e ready
pris/e taken
privé private
le **prix** price
prochain/e next
proche near
profond/e deep
puis then
le **pull** sweater

Q

le **quai** platform
quand when
que that; what; whom
qu'est-ce que c'est? what is it?
qui who, which

R

ralentir to slow down
la **randonnée** walk
le **rappel** reminder
RC / rez-de-chaussée ground floor (US 1st)
le **reçu** receipt
remplir to fill
le **rendez-vous** appointment
les **renseignements** *mpl* information
réparer to repair
le **repas** meal
rester to remain/stay
revenir to come back
le **rideau** curtain
rien nothing; **de ~** don't mention it
le **risque** risk
les **riverains** *mpl* residents
la **rivière** river
le **robinet** tap/faucet
le **rond-point** roundabout
rose pink
la **rôtisserie** steakhouse
la **roue** wheel
rouge red
la **route nationale** main road
la **rue** street

S

la **salle** room; ~ **à manger** dining ~; ~ **de bains** bath-~; ~ **de réunion** meeting ~
samedi Saturday
s'appeler to be called
le **sac** bag; ~ **de couchage** sleeping bag; ~ **à dos** rucksack
le **salon** lounge
sans without
sauf except
le **secours** help; first aid
le **séjour** stay
la **semaine** week
sentir to smell; feel
septembre September
serrez à droite keep to the right
la **serrure** lock
service compris service included
seul alone; **~-ement** only
le **soir** evening
solaire for the sun; le **soleil** sun
la **sortie (de secours)** (emergency) exit
sortir to go out
le **sous-sol** basement
les **spiritueux** *mpl* spirits (drinks)
le **stade** stadium
la **station-service** petrol station
stationnement interdit no parking
le **sud** south
sur on
les **surgelés** *mpl* frozen food
svp - s'il vous plaît please

T

le **tabac** tobacco/tobacconist's
tard late
le **tarif** tarif, rate
le **taux** rate
le **temps** weather; time (general)

la **tête** head
le **timbre** stamp
tirer to pull
le **tour** trip; la **tour** tower
le **tournoi** tournament
tous *mpl* **toutes** *fpl* all
tout/e everything/ all (s.); ~ **compris** all inclusive
tout de suite at once; **tout droit** straight on
la **toux** cough
travailler to work
le **traveller** traveller's cheque
traverser to cross
très very
trop too; ~ **de** too much
trouver to find; **se ~** to be situated

V

les **vacances** *fpl* holidays
le **vélo** bicycle
vendre to sell
vendredi Friday
venir to come
le **verre** glass
vert/e green
le **vestiaire** cloakroom
vieux/vieille old
la **ville** town
le **virage dangereuse** dangerous bend
le **visage** face
vite quick/ly
voilà there/here it is
voir to see
le **vol** flight; theft

Y

les **yeux** *mpl* eyes

English-French and Index

A

a/an un *m*, une *f*, des *pl* 94
about environ 86
abroad l'étranger *m* 72
to **accept** accepter 48
accident l'accident *m* 67,79
address l'adresse *f* 52,91
to **adjust** régler 70
adult l'adulte *m/f* 7
in **advance** à l'avance *f* 61
aeroplane l'avion *m* 78
after après 81
afternoon l'après-midi 57,86,92
again encore, de nouveau 58

age l'âge *m* 7,80,87
agent l'agent *m* 60
... **ago** il y a ...
air l'air *m* 70,78; **~-conditioning** la climatisation
airport l'aéroport *m* 52,78
all tout/e, tous/toutes 13,37,48,55
allergic to allergique à 81
alphabet 52
already déjà
also aussi
always toujours
ambulance l'ambulance *f* 79
American américain/e 90

and et 9
annual annuel/le 61
another un/e autre; ~ **one** encore
  un/une 9,22
antifreeze l'antigel *m*
antiseptic cream la crème antiseptique
  45
anything else autre chose 27,36
apartment l'appartement *m*
appendix l'appendice *m* 82
appointment le rendez-vous 56,57,79
approximately environ 86
arm le bras 82
arrival l'arrivée *f* 72,78
to **ask** demander
aspirin l'aspirine *f* 45
assembly *(product)* la fabrication 60
asthmatic asthmatique 81
attacked attaqué/e 91
Australia l'Australie *f* 90
available disponible; **not** ~ absent/e 55
awning l'auvent *m* 7

B
baby le bébé; ~ **food** les aliments pour
  bébé 45
back le dos 82
bad mauvais/e 28
bag le sac 91; ~**s** bagages *mpl* 72,78
baggage lockers la consigne 72
baker's la boulangerie 37
ball la balle 84
bandage la bande velpeau 45
Band-Aid les pansements *mpl* 45
bank la banque 49; ~ **account** le
  compte bancaire 61
banker's card la carte bancaire 48,61
bar le bar 22,23
batch le lot 60
bath le bain 10; ~**-room** la salle de
  bains 7,17
battery la pile 43; *(car)* la batterie 68
to **be/be able** être/pouvoir 90,95
beach la plage 62
beautiful beau *m*, belle *f*
because parce que bc
bed le lit 10; ~**-room** la chambre à
  coucher 16
beef le boeuf 30,38
bee l'abeille *f*
beer la bière 23,42
before avant (de) 81
beginner le/la débutant/e 85
behind derrière 64
Belgium la Belgique 3,90
belt la ceinture 46
bend le virage; **bent** tordu/e 70

better meilleur/e; (the) **best** (le/la)
  mieux 12
bicycle le vélo, la bicyclette 65; ~ **parts**
  68-69; **by** ~ à vélo
big grand/e 7, 36, 47; ~**-er** plus grand/e
bill l'addition *f*, la note *(hotel)* 13;
  (restaurant) 22,24,28; *(shops)* 37,48
bindings *(ski)* les fixations *fpl* 85
bird l'oiseau *m*
biscuits les biscuits *m* 42
a **bit** un peu 36
bite la piqûre 44; **bitten** mordu/e 44,80
blanket la couverture 16
blister l'ampoule *f*
blocked bloqué/e 15
blood le sang 80; ~**-pressure** la
  tension 81
blouse le chemisier 46
boarding l'embarquement *m* 78
boat le bateau 76-77; **by** ~ en bateau
body le corps 82
boiler la chaudière 17
book le livre 43
to **book** réserver 8
booking *(entertainment)* 86; *(hotel)* 7,
  8–11; *(camping)* 7,20; *(meal)* 26;
  (travel) 74-76,78
bookshop le librairie 43
to **borrow** emprunter 14
bottle la bouteille 29; ~**-opener** le
  décapsuleur 43
bowl le bol 19
box la boîte
boy le garçon 90
branch office la succursale 60
bread le pain 25,37
to **break** casser; **broken** cassé/e 15
breakdown; I've broken down je suis
  en panne 67
breakfast le petit déjeuner 13,25
bridge le pont 62
briefs le slip 46
to **bring back** rendre, ramener 71
Britain la Grande Bretagne 50,90
brochure la brochure 60,83
brother le frère 87
builder un entrepreneur 15
bulb l'ampoule *f* 16,68
bus le bus, l'autobus 75; ~ **station** la
  gare routière 75; ~ **stop** l'arrêt *m* 75
business les affaires *fpl* 54-61; **to do** ~
  faire des affaires 57
but mais
butcher's la boucherie 38
butter le beurre 25,42
button le bouton 66
to **buy** acheter 43

C

cable le câble 68
cabin la cabine 76
café le café 22,23
cake la pâtisserie, le gâteau
to **call** appeler 51,55,78,79; **I'm called** je m'appelle *(s'appeler)* 87
calm calm/e 77
camera l'appareil-photo *m*
camp,-ing 7,20-21; ~ **Gaz** 20; **~-site** le camping 7,20
I **can/can** I je peux/puis-je *(pouvoir)* 52,58,83,bc
can (tin) la boîte; ~ **opener** l'ouvre-boîtes *m* 43
Canada le Canada 90
canal le canal 76
to **cancel** annuler 66,78
capable capable 60
car la voiture 65,67; ~ **hire** location de voitures 71; ~ **park** le parking 8,66; ~ **parts** 68-69; **by** ~ en voiture
caravan la caravane 7,20
card *(visiting)* la carte de visite 56
carpenter le menuisier 15
cash - desk la caisse 48,49; ~ **dispenser** le distributeur de billets 49
castle le château 62,83
Casualty Department Urgences 80
cat le chat
cathedral la cathédrale 62
ceiling le plafond 16
central heating le chauffage central 17
cereal *(breakfast)* la céréale 42
chair la chaise 19
chair lift le télésiège
chandlery le magasin d'accastillage 77
to **change** changer 48,49,66,76,78
the **Channel** la Manche 63; ~ **tunnel** le tunnel sous la Manche 63
charge le prix 60,86
cheaper moins cher 12
check/bill la note, l'addition *f* 13,22,28
check-in l'enregistrement *m* 78
cheers! (à votre) santé! 22
cheese le fromage 42
chemist's la pharmacie 44
cheque le chèque 61
chest la poitrine 82
chicken le poulet 30,38
child l'enfant *m/f* 7,10,20,28,83,90
chimney la cheminée 14
chips/fries les frites *fpl* 27
chocolate le chocolat 25,29
choice le choix 24,61
chop la côtelette 38
Christmas Noël *m* 93
church l'église *f* 62

cigarette la cigarette 43
cinema le cinéma 62,86
clean propre
close to près de 64
to **close** fermer; **closed** fermé/e 21,36,77
clothes les vêtements *mpl* 46-48
coach le car 75
coat le manteau 46
coffee le café 23, 25
coffee pot la cafetière 19
coke le coca 23
cold froid/e 23; **I'm/it's** ~ j'ai/il fait froid 17,93; **I've got a** ~ je suis enrhumé/e
colleague le/la collègue 58
to **collect** ramasser
colour la couleur fc,47,85
comb le peigne 45
to **come** venir, arriver 79,88; ~ **in!** entrez!; ~ **off** partir 15
comfortable confortable
commission la commission 61
company la société 55,56
complaint la réclamation 28,48
component le composant 60
computer l'ordinateur *m* 59
concert le concert 86
condom le préservatif 45
conference room la salle de réunion
to **confirm** confirmer 66
connection la correspondance 72,76
constipation la constipation 44
contract le contrat 61
to be **convenient** convenir 57
to **cook** faire cuire; **cooker** la cuisinière 18
cookies les biscuits *mpl* 42
corkscrew le tire-bouchon 43
corner le coin 64
cost le prix; **to** ~ coûter 15,36,52,bc
costs les frais 61
cot le lit d'enfant 10
cotton *(material)* le coton; ~ **thread** le fil 43; **~-wool** le coton (hydrophile) 45
couchette la couchette 74
cough la toux 44
could I/you pourrais-je/pourriez-vous 14, 58
country le pays 90; **~-side** la campagne
of **course** bien sûr 12
cover charge le couvert
cracked fendu/e 15
crash la collision 67; ~ **helmet** le casque
cream la crème 45
credit card la carte bancaire 13,48
crisps les chips *mpl*
to **cross** traverser; **~-roads** le carrefour 64
crossing la traversée 76
cup la tasse 14,19,22;
cupboard le placard 16

(in local) currency en (monnaie) locale 61
current le courant 77
curtain le rideau 16; **~ rail** la tringle à
  rideaux 16
customs la douane 77
to **cut** couper
cystitis la cystite

D

daily, every day tous les jours 72
damp humide
to **dance** danser 89
danger danger,; **~-ous** ~-eux/euse 77
date la date 61; **~-stamping tickets** 73
daughter la fille 87
day le jour, la journée 9,71,83,84,86; *(of
week)* 92
dear cher/chère 47
decaffeinated décaféiné/e 23
deck le pont
decorator le décorateur 15
to **decide** décider
delicatessen l'épicerie *f*, le traiteur 38
delicious délicieux/-euse 89
delighted heureux/-euse 58
delivery la livraison 61
dentist le dentiste 81
deodorant le déodorant 45
departure le départ 72,78
deposit les arrhes *fpl* 7; la caution
dessert le dessert 27
detergent la lessive 42
diabetic diabétique 81
to **dial** composer 51
diaper la couche 45
diarrhoea la diarrhée 44
dictionary le dictionnaire 43
diesel le gazole 70,77
different différent/e
difficult difficile
dining room la salle à manger
dinner le dîner 13,22
direct direct/e 78; **~ion** la direction
63,64
director le directeur 54
dirty sale 28
disabled handicapé/e 7
disco la discothèque 86
discount la remise 61
dishwasher le lave-vaisselle 18
disk la disquette 59
to **disturb** déranger
distributor le distributeur 60; *(car)* 68
diversion *(road)* le déviation 65
divorced divorcé/e
to **do** faire 88,91
doctor le docteur 79
dog le chien

dollar le dollar 48
door la porte 14
double double 7,10
drain l'égout *m* 14; **~-pipe** le tuyau
d'évacuation 14
dreadful affreux/affreuse
dress la robe 46
dressing (medical) le pansement 44
drink la boisson 29; **to ~** boire 29,88,89
to **drip** goutter
driving licence le permis de conduire 71
drugstore la pharmacie 44
dry sec/sèche; **~-cleaner's** le pressing
dustbin la poubelle 19
dustpan & brush la pelle et le balai 19
duvet la couette 16

E

each chaque 36; **~ one** chacun
ear l'oreille *f* 82
earache les douleurs d'oreille 44
early tôt
east l'est *m* 63
Easter Pâques 93
easy facile
to **eat** manger 80
egg l'oeuf *m* 42
elbow le coude
electric électrique; **electrician**
l'électricien *m* 15; **electricity**
l'électricité *f* 7,17,21,68
email email 59
embassy l'ambassade *f*
emergencies 44,51,67,79
empty vide
end la fin
engaged *(occupied)* occupé/e 54,64
engine le moteur 68
England l'Angleterre *f* 50,90; **English**
anglais/e 43,90, bc
to **enjoy** 27
enough assez 36
entertainment 86
entrance l'entrée *f* 83
envelope l'enveloppe *f*
epileptic épileptique 81
equipment l'équipement *m*
especially surtout
estate agent l'agent *m* immobilier
estimate le devis 61
evening le soir 26,86,92
every *(each)* chaque; *(all)* tous/toute
36,66,72,83
except sauf 36,73
excursion l'excursion *f*
excuse me excusez-moi 24,bc
exhibition l'exposition *f* 83
exit la sortie 72

expensive cher/chère 12,47
to **explain** expliquer
export l'exportation f; **to ~** exporter
expressway l'autoroute f 65
extension no. le numéro de poste 54
extra en supplément 13,22
eye l'oeil m, pl les yeux 82

F

face le visage
factory l'usine f
to **fall** tomber; **fall** (season) l'automne m 93
family la famille 7,10,90
fantastic fantastique
far loin; **as ~ as** jusqu'à 64
father le père 90
faucet le robinet 17
favourite préféré/e
fax le fax 59
I'm fed up j'en ai eu assez
to **feel** sentir; **I feel** je me sens
fence la clôture, la barrière 14
ferry le bac, le ferry 76
festival la fête
fill it up le plein 70
film (camera) la pellicule 43; (movie) le film 86
filter le filtre 43
finance la finance 61
to **find** trouver 52; **~ a seat** 22; **~ the way** 64
fine très bien, bien/parfait 9,12,87,bc
finger le doigt
to **finish** finir 86
finished products les produits finis 60
fire la cheminée 16; **~ brigade** les pompiers mpl 14,51
firm la compagnie
First Aid 79
first premier/première 12,64,88,112
fish le poisson 27,39; **~ing** pêcher 84
fit me (it doesn't) ça ne me va pas 47
flashlight la lampe de poche 43
flat (apartment) l'appartement m ; (tyre) la crevaison 69
flavour (ice cream) le parfum 29
flight le vol 78
floor l'étage m, le sol 12,16,56; **~-cloth** la serpillière 19
flour la farine
flower la fleur
fly la mouche
foggy (it's) il fait du brouillard
food la nourriture
foot le pied 82; **on ~** à pied 65
football le football/foot 86
footpath le sentier

for pour 27
forest la forêt, le bois 62
to **forget** oublier
fork la fourchette 19,22
form le formulaire 91
a **fortnight** quinze jours
forward en avant; **to look ~** 57
France la France; **French** français/e 3,43,88,90,bc
free gratuit/e; (vacant) libre 22,55,57,66,83,88
freezer le congélateur 18
fresh frais/fraîche
fridge le frigo 18
fried frit/e
my **friend** mon ami/e 87
fries les frites fpl 27
frightened effrayé/e
from de
in **front (of)** devant 64
fruit le fruit 41; **~ juice** le jus de fruits 23,42
frying pan la poêle 19
fuel (petrol) 70,77; (gas,electricity) 17
full plein/e 70; **~ up** complet/complète 9
fuse le fusible 17,68

G

game le jeu; (match) le match 84
garage le garage 67
garden le jardin 14
gas le gaz 17; **camping ~** 20; (car) l'essence f 70; **~ station** 70
Germany l'Allemagne f 90
to **get** trouver, obtenir 77; **~ off** descendre 75; **~ to** pour aller à 64
girl la jeune fille 90; **~-friend** l'amie f 87
to **give** donner 54,55
glass le verre 19,22
glasses les lunettes fpl
gloves les gants mpl 46
gluten-free sans gluten
to **go** aller 74,75,86,95; **~ away!** allez-vous-en! 91; **~ in** entrer 83; **~ out** sortir
golf le golf 84
good bon/ne; bien 11,47
goodbye au revoir 13,36,89,92,bc
good morning etc bonjour 36,92,bc
grass l'herbe f
grateful reconnaissant/e 15,59
greasy gras/se 35
great! super!
Great Britain la Grande-Bretagne 50,88,90
green vert/e fc; **~ card** la carte verte
greetings 92,bc

grilled grillé/e
grocer's l'épicerie f 36,42
ground floor le rez de chaussée 12
group le groupe
guide le guide 83

H

hair les cheveux mpl; ~ dryer le sèche-cheveux 18
half demi/e; la moitié 36,53
ham le jambon 23,38
hamburger le hamburger
hammer le marteau
hand la main 82; ~-bag le sac 91; ~-kerchief le mouchoir 45
handicapped handicapé/e 7
happy heureux/-euse 57,58
harbour le port 77; ~ master's office la capitainerie 77
hat le chapeau; woolly ~ le bonnet 46
I have j'ai (avoir) 8,9,36,95; I ~ to je dois (devoir) 95
hay fever le rhume des foins 44
he il 14,80,95
head la tête 82; ~-ache le mal de tête 44; ~ office le siège social 60
heart le coeur 81,82
heating le chauffage 17
hello bonjour, salut 8,87,92,bc
helmet le casque
help l'aide f, aider; 'au secours' 14;56,67,79,89,91,bc
here ici 64
high haut/e
hill la colline
to hire louer; location 69,71,84,85
hobby le hobby 89
hold on! ne quittez pas! 54
hole le trou 15
(on) holiday (en) vacances fpl ; public ~ 50
to go home rentrer
honey le miel 42
to hope espérer; I hope so (not) j'espère que oui (non)
horrible affreux/affreuse
horse le cheval; ~-riding l'équitation f 84
hospital l'hôpital m 79
hot chaud/e 17,25,93; (spicy) épicé/e
hotel l'hôtel m 7,8-13
hour l'heure f 84
house la maison 14; at my ~ chez moi; at your ~ chez vous
how comment; ~ are you comment allez-vous 87, bc; ~ long combien de temps 15,70,71,80,88; ~ many/much combien 9,15,36,52,70,84,bc
I'm hungry j'ai faim 22 (avoir)

I'm hurt j'ai mal 80,81,82 (avoir)
husband le mari 87
hypermarket l'hypermarché m 36

I

I je 95
ice, ~ cream la glace 29,67,77; ~ cubes les glaçons mpl 23
if si
ill malade 79,81
immediately tout de suite
important important/e
impossible impossible
in/into dans 91
included compris/e 13,17
industry l'industrie f
infected infecté/e
information les renseignements mpl 60,72,83
insect, ~ bite la piqûre d'insecte 44; ~repellant la crème anti-insecte 45
inside (of) à l'intérieur (de)
instead of au lieu de
insulin l'insuline f 81
insurance l'assurance f 71
interest (rate) (le taux d') intérêt 61
interesting intéressant/e 83
international international/e
to introduce présenter 58,87
to invite inviter 88
invoice la facture 61
Ireland l'Irlande; Irish irlandais/e 90
iron le fer à repasser 18
is (to be) être 95,bc; is it? est-ce, est-il/elle? 13,22,95
island l'île f 62
Italy l'Italie f 90

J

jacket la veste
jam la confiture 25,42
jeans le jean 46
job le travail
(good) journey (bon) voyage m 65
jug le pot 19
juice le jus 23,42
just (only) seulement

K

key la clé 11,14,69
kilo le kilo 36,39; ~ metre le kilomètre
kitchen la cuisine 18-19
knee le genou
knickers le slip 46
knife le couteau 19,22
I know je sais (savoir) bc; (person) je connais (connaître)

L

ladder l'échelle *f* 14
lager la bière blonde 23
lake le lac 62
lamb l'agneau *m*, le mouton 30,38
lamp la lampe 16,69
to **land** atterrir
last dernier/e 74,78,85
late tard; **later** plus tard 14
lavatory les toilettes *fpl* 10,17,24,64
leak la fuite; **to ~** fuire 15,17,69
to **learn** apprendre; **I learn** j'apprends
at **least** au moins
to **leave** partir 88
(to the) left (à) gauche 64; **~ luggage
   office** la consigne 72
leg la jambe 82
less moins
lesson la leçon 85
letter la lettre 59
life, ~-belt la ceinture; **~-jacket** le gilet
   de sauvetage 76
lift l'ascenseur *m* 12,56,85
light la lampe, la lumière 16,69; **~ bulb**
   l'ampoule *f* 16, 68; **~ switch**
   l'interrupteur *m* 17
lighter le briquet 43
to **like** aimer, vouloir 13,27,37,54,88,89,bc;
   I'd ~ je voudrais; **~ that** comme ça 37
line la ligne 60,76
list la liste 60,83
little petit/e; **a ~** un peu (de) 36,88,89
to **live** habiter 14,88
living room le salon 16
locations 64
lock la serrure; l'écluse 14,76,77; **to
   ~**fermer à clé
long long/longue 9,75; **a ~ time**
   longtemps
to **look at** regarder; **~ for** chercher 14;
   ~forward 57,58; **~ like** 91
I'm just looking je regarde seulement 36
loose desserré/e 15
to **lose** perdre; **lost** perdu/e 72,91,bc
lost property objets trouvés 72
loud fort/e
lovely agréable 89
LPG *(fuel)* le GPL 70
luggage les bagages *mpl* 69,72,78
lunch le déjeuner 13,22

M

machine la machine 60
mail la poste 50
make *(brand)* la marque 67; **to ~** faire
   81
man l'homme *m* 64

manager le directeur 54; **export/sales
   ~** directeur export/des ventes 54
many beaucoup (de); **not ~** pas
   beaucoup (de)
map la carte 43,76,83
margarine la margarine 42
marina le port de plaisance 76
market le marché 62
married marié/e
match *(game)* le match 86
matches les allumettes *fpl* 43
matter (what's the) 70,bc
me moi 90; **to ~** me 7,90,bc
meal le repas 13,27; **~ times** 22;
   enjoy your ~ bon appétit 22
to **mean** bc
measure/s 39,47
meat la viande 27,38
mechanic le mécanicien 77
medicine le médicament 44,45,80,81
medium moyen/ne 71
to **meet** rencontrer 57; **~ again** revoir **~ing**
   la réunion 55,87,88; **~-room** la salle de
   réunion
membership card la carte d'adhérent 21
to **mend** réparer 15
menu la carte; **set ~** le menu 22,30-35
message le message 55
meter le compteur 17; *(length)* le mètre
metro le métro 76
microwave le four à micro-ondes 18
mid-day midi; **~-night** minuit 53
milk le lait 23,25,42; **~ shake** le
   milkshake 23
mirror le miroir
to **miss** rater 74,78
mistake l'erreur *f* 28
moment le moment 26
money l'argent *m* 48,49,66,91
month le mois 66,93
more plus (de) 14,36,89; **no ~** il n'y a
   plus 17
morning le matin 57,92
mosquito le moustique
mother la mère 90
motor le moteur 69; **~ caravan** le
   camping-car 20; **~-cycle** la moto 65;
   (parts) 68-69
motorway l'autoroute *f* 65
mountain la montagne
mouth la bouche 82
movie le film 62,86
Mr, Mrs monsieur, madame 13,23,57
much beaucoup;**not ~** pas beaucoup 21
museum le musée 83
music la musique 89
one **must** il faut 54,80

mustard la moutarde 42
my mon/ma/mes 94

N

nail le clou
name le nom 8,26,54,87,91
nappy la couche 45
nationality la nationalité 90
near (to) près (de) 9,64; **~-est** le/la
  plus proche 51,70
nearly presque
necessary nécessaire 15,58
neck le cou
to **need** il faut, avoir besoin de 14,54,68,79
needle l'aiguille *f* 43
nerve le nerf 82
never jamais
New Zealand la Nouvelle Zélande 90
newspaper le journal 43
next prochain/e 74,78
new nouveau/nouvelle
nice agréable, bon/ne 27,88,89;
  (person) sympathique
night la nuit/nuitée 7,9,21,92
no non, pas de; **not** ne...pas
  37,72,80,88,bc
nobody personne
noise le bruit; **noisy** bruyant/e 12
non-alcoholic non-alcoolisé/e 89
north le nord 63
not at all je vous en prie, de rien 48,55
nothing rien 48
now maintenant 14,67,92
number le numéro 11,47,51,112
nut la noix; l'écrou *m* 28, 69

O

occupied occupé/e 22,73
of de
of course bien sûr 12
off *(turned)* fermé/e, éteint/e 17
office le bureau 56
often souvent 75
oil l'huile *f* 4270
OK OK, d'accord bc
old vieux/vielle; âge 80,83,87
on sur; **to turn ~** ouvrir; allumer 17
once une fois
one way aller simple; sens unique 65,74
only seulement
open ouvert/e; **to ~** ouvrir 36,77,83
in my **opinion** à mon avis
opposite to en face de 64
order la commande 61; **out of ~** hors
  service 64
other autre 9
out *(he/she is ~)* il/elle est sorti/e,
  absent/e 55

outboard motor le moteur hors-bord 76
outside dehors, en plein air
to **overheat** chauffer 68
to **owe** devoir 70,80

P

pan la casserole 18
pannier la sacoche 69
paper le papier
pardon pardon
parent le parent 90
park le jardin, le parc 62
parking meter le parcmètre 66
party la fête
passenger le passager 78
passport le passeport 8,49,91
pasta les pâtes *fpl* 42
path le chemin
to **pay** payer 13,24,28,48
pen, pencil le stylo, le crayon 43
pensioner la personne âgée, retraité/e
  83,88
people les gens *mpl*
perhaps peut-être
period *(woman's)* les règles *fpl*
person la personne 9,20,26
permit le permis 84
pests 91
petrol l'essence *f* 70; **~ station** la
  station-service 70
pharmacy la pharmacie 44
photograph la photo 43
photocopie la photocopie 59
picture l'image *f*
piece le morceau 36
pillow l'oreiller *m* 16; **~-case** la taie
  d'oreiller 16
pilot light la veilleuse 17
pitch l'emplacement *m* 7,20
place names 3,88
plan *(town)* le plan 64,83
plane l'avion *m* 78; **by ~** en avion
plasters les pansements *mpl* 45
plate l'assiette *f* 19
platform le quai, la voie 74
to **play** jouer 84
pleasant agréable
pleasantries 58
please s'il vous plaît 49; **~-d to meet**
  enchanté/e 87,89,bc
plug *(electric)* la prise de courant 17
plumber le plombier 15; **plumbing** 17
pocket la poche
police station le poste de police
  62,67,91
pop concert le concert pop 86
pork le porc 30,38

port le port 77; *(side)* bâbord 76; ~ **of registry** port d'immatriculation 77
possible possible 81
post box la boîte aux lettres; ~-**card** la carte postale 43; ~ **office** la poste 50
to prefer préférer
pregnant enceinte 81
prescription l'ordonnance *f* 80
pretty joli/e
price le prix 86; **inclusive** ~ le prix forfaitaire 61; ~ **list** la liste de prix 60
priority to right la priorité à droite 65,67
problem le problème 15,28,78,91
to process traiter 60
product le produit 60
production line la ligne de fabrication 60
profit le profit
programme *(computer)* le logiciel 59
projector le rétroprojecteur 59
public holidays les jours fériés *mpl* 50
publicity material la documentation 60
pump la pompe 69
to punch tickets composter 73
puncture la crevaison 69

Q

quantities 36,39
quay le quai 76
queries 28;
question la question 95
quickly vite 79
quiet tranquille 12
quite assez 36
quotation le devis 61

R

racket *(tennis)* la raquette 84
radiator le radiateur 69
radio la radio
rain la pluie 93
range *(products)* la gamme 60
rate le tarif 7
raw materials les matières premières *fpl* 60
razor le rasoir 45
to read lire; **reading** la lecture 89
receipt le reçu 13,48,52
to receive recevoir 57
reception la réception
to recommend recommander 15,83
reduction la réduction 83
to refund rembourser 48
to repair réparer 15,70
refrigerator le frigo 18
registration number le numéro d'immatriculation 8
relations *(family)* 87,90
I remember je me rappelle *(se rappeler)*

to rent louer 71
to repeat répéter bc
reply la réponse
representative le représentant 60
requests 14,58
reservations - *see* booking
retired retraité/e 83,88
restaurant le restaurant 26-29
result le résultat
to return (bring back) ramener 71; ~ **ticket** aller-retour *m* 71,74
rice le riz 42
to go riding faire du cheval 84
to ring back rappeler 55
to the right (à) droite 64; **to be** ~ avoir raison
river la rivière 63
road la route 63; ~ **signs** 65-67
to rob voler 91
roof le toit 14,15
roll le petit pain 25,37
room la chambre 8,12,16
rope la corde 43
round trip aller-retour *m* 74
roundabout le rond-point 64
rubbish les ordures *fpl* 14
rucksack le sac à dos

S

safe sans danger
sailing la voile 76-77,84
salad la salade
sales les soldes *mpl* 47; ~ **volume** le volume des ventes
salt le sel 42; **salty** salé/e
same le/la même
sandwich le sandwich 23
sanitary napkin/towel la serviette hygiénique 45
Saturday samedi 66,88,92
saucepan la casserole 18
saucer la soucoupe 18
sausages les saucisses *fpl* 38
to say dire
school l'école *f*
scissors les ciseaux *mpl* 43
Scotland l'Écosse *f* 90; **Scottish** écossais/e
screw la vis 69; ~-**driver** le tournevis 69
sea la mer 77; ~-**sickness** le mal de mer 44
seafood les fruits *m* de mer 39
season la saison 93
seat la place 22,74
second second/e, deuxième 112
to see voir 12,57,83

self,~-catering 14-19; ~-service libre-
service 24,70
to **sell** vendre 50
to **send** envoyer 59,60
septic tank la fosse septique 14
service included service compris
several plusieurs
shade l'ombrage *m* 7,
shampoo le shampooing 45
shaving, ~-cream la crème à raser 45;
~ **point** la prise pour rasoir 17
she elle 14,80,95
sheet le drap 16,21
shirt la chemise 46
shoes les chaussures *fpl* 46,85
shop le magasin 62; **to go shopping**
faire des courses; ~ **centre** le centre
commercial 36
short court/e; **shorts** le short 46
to **show** montrer 15
shower la douche 7,10,17
to **shut** fermer 17; **shut** fermé/e 36
shutters les volets *mpl* 16
sick malade; **to be ~** vomir 44,80
side le côté
sightseeing le tourisme 83
to **sign** signer 8,49
since depuis
single pour une personne 7,10; *(ticket)*
aller simple *m* 74
sink l'évier *m* 18
sister la soeur 87
sit down! asseyez-vous! 89
size *(clothes)* la taille 47; *(shoes)* la
pointure 85
skates les patins *m* à glace 85
to **go skiing** faire du ski 85
skirt la jupe 46
sledge la luge 85
to **sleep** dormir; ~-**ing bag** le sac de
couchage 21
slice la tranche 36
slow lent; ~**ly** lentement *bc*
small petit/e 7,36,47, 1
smell l'odeur *f* 28; **to ~** sentir
to **smoke** fumer 43,74
snacks 23
snail l'escargot *m* 39
snake le serpent 80
snow la neige 93; ~-**board** le snowboard 85; ~ **chains** les chaînes de
neige 69
so si; **like this** comme ça 37
soap le savon 45; ~ **powder** la lessive
42
socks les chaussettes *fpl* 46
socket la prise (femelle) 17

soft drink la boisson non alcoolisée
23,89
software le logiciel 59
some,-one quelqu'un/e 15,59; ~-**thing**
quelque chose; ~-**times** de temps en
temps
son le fils 87
soon bientôt 89,bc; **as ~ as possible**
aussitôt que possible 81
sort le genre 71
sorry (pardon me) pardon; **I'm ~** je suis
désolé/e, je regrette 12,36,55,bc
soup la soupe
south le sud 63
Spain l'Espagne *f* 90
spanner la clef à écrous 69
to **speak** parler 54,bc
speciality la specialité
speed limit la limitation de vitesse 65
to **spell/write** épeler, écrire 52,55
spoon la cuillère 18,22
sport le sport 84-85,89
spring le printemps 93
square la place 49
staff *(talking to)* 14,15
stairs l'escalier *m* 16
to **stall** caler 68
stamp le timbre 43,50
starboard tribord 76
to **start** commencer 86
statement of account le relevé de
compte 61
station la gare 52,72-73,75
stay le séjour; **to ~** rester 7,88,91
steak le bifteck 27
to **steal** voler; **stolen** volé/e 91
sticky tape le ruban adhésif
stomach l'estomac *m* 44; ~ **ache** les
douleurs d'estomac 44
stone la pierre
stop l'arrêt *m* 75; **to ~** arrêter
stopcock le robinet d'arrêt 17
stove la cuisinière 18
straight droit/e; ~ **on** tout droit 64
strap la sangle 69
straw la paille
street la rue 63,64
string la ficelle 43
strong fort/e
stuck coincé/e 70
student l'étudiant/e *m/f* 83,88;
to **study** – faire des études de –
stung piqué/e 80
subsidiary la filiale 60
subway *(train)* le métro 76
sugar le sucre 42
summer l'été *m* 93

sun le soleil; **~-burn** les coups de soleil 44; **~-glasses** les lunettes *fpl* de soleil 45; **~-tan oil** l'huile *f* solaire 45
Sunday dimanche 66,92
supermarket le supermarché 36
sure sûr/e
surfing le surf; **~-board** la planche à voile 84
sweater le pull 46
sweets les bonbons *mpl* 37
to **swim** nager 84
swimming costume/trunks le maillot 46; **~ pool** la piscine 84
switch l'interrupteur *m*, le bouton; **to ~ off** éteindre; **to ~ on** allumer 17
Switzerland la Suisse 3,90

T

table la table 19,26
to **take** prendre 48,64,70,75; **taken** occupé/e 22,64; **~ place** 78
tampon le tampon 45
tap le robinet 17
tarif le tarif 7
taste le goût 89
tax la taxe 13; **before ~** hors taxes 61
taxi le taxi 52
tea le thé 23,42; **~-pot** la théière 19; **~ spoon** la petite cuillère 19; **~ towel** le torchon 19
telephone le téléphone 51,54-55,67;
to **~** téléphoner; **~ directory** l'annuaire *m*
to **tell** dire 7,75
temperature la température, la fièvre 80,81
tennis le tennis 84
tent la tente 7,20
tetanus le tétanos 80
thank you (very much) merci (beaucoup/bien) 11,13,55,88,89,bc
thanking people 14,15
the le *m*, la *f*, les *pl* 94
theatre le théâtre 63,86
theft 91
there là; **~ you are** voilà 37,64
there is/are il y a 17,bc
they ils/elles 95
thing la chose
I **think so/not** je pense que oui/non
I'm **thirsty** j'ai soif *(avoir)* 22
this/that ça, ce/cette; **these** ces 24,36,87,94
this one, that one ceci, cela 36
thread le fil 43
throat la gorge 82; **sore ~** le mal de gorge 44
ticket le billet 72-76,78; *(entertainment)* 86; *(punching)* 72; *(buying)* 74

tide le courant; **high ~** haute mer 77
tights les collants *mpl* 46
tile la tuile 14
time l'heure 13,26,53,56,66,83,88,89,92; **how many ~s** combien de fois
timetable l'horaire *m* 72
tin la boîte; **~ opener** l'ouvre-boîtes *m* 43
tipping 22,52
tired fatigué/e
to à *(part of verbs p.96)*
toast le toast
today aujourd'hui 14,92
toe l'orteil *m* 82
together ensemble 57
toilet les toilettes *fpl* 10,24,64; **~ paper** le papier hygiénique 42
toiletries 45
toll le péage 65
tomorrow demain 14,57,86,92
tonight ce soir 9,21,86,88,92
too *(also)* aussi; *(much)* trop 47
tool l'outil *m* 69
tooth,-ache le mal au dents 81; **~-brush** la brosse à dents 45; **~-paste** le dentifrice 45
torch la lampe de poche 43
total le total 61
tourist office l'office *m* de tourisme 9,63,83
to **tow** remorquer
towards vers
towel la serviette 17
town la ville 63,83; **~ centre** le centre-ville 62; **~ hall** la mairie 63
toy le jouet
traffic lights les feux *mpl* 64
train le train 72-74,76; **by ~** en train
to **translate** traduire
transfer *(money)* le virement 61
trash les poubelles *fpl* 14
to **travel** voyager; **~ agency** l'agence *f* de voyages
traveller's cheque le travellers 13,48,49,91
tree l'arbre *m*
trip le voyage 65; **have a good ~** bon voyage 65
trousers le pantalon 46
true vrai; **that's ~** c'est vrai
to **try** essayer 47
T-shirt le T-shirt 46
tunnel le tunnel 63; **Channel ~** le tunnel sous la Manche 63
turkey la dinde, le dindon 30,38
to **turn** tourner; **~ off/on** fermer/ouvrir 17
turnover le chiffre d'affaires 61

TV la télé 18; ~ **aerial** l'antenne de ~
twice deux fois
to **type** taper 59

U

umbrella le parapluie
uncomfortable inconfortable
under sous
underground *(train)* le métro 76
underpants le slip 46
I **understand** je comprends bc
unfortunately malheureusement
university l'université f
unlimited illimité 71
until jusqu'à
urgent urgent/e 79,81
urine l'urine f 80
USA les Etats-Unis 50,90
to **use** utiliser 58; **useful** utile
usually normalement

V

vacant libre 9,64
vaccinated vacciné/e 80
vacuum cleaner l'aspirateur 18
valley la vallée 63
valve la valve 69
VAT TVA 61
vegetables les légumes *mpl* 24,38,40-41
vegetarian végétarien/ne 28
very très 47; ~ **much** très bien/beaucoup 88,bc
video la vidéo 18
village le village
vinegar le vinaigre
visit la visite; **to** ~ visiter 83,89
vitamin la vitamine

W

to **wait (for)** attendre
Wales le Pays de Galles; **Welsh** gallois/e 90
walk la promenade; la randonnée 83; **to** ~ marcher 65
wall le mur 14
wallet le portefeuille
I **want** je veux *(vouloir)* 13
warm chaud/e 17,93
to **wash** laver 18,20
washing,-machine le lave-linge 18
~**-powder** la lessive 42; ~**-up liquid** le liquide pour la vaisselle 42
wasp la guêpe
watch la montre
water l'eau f 17,29,42,70,77; ~ **heater** le chauffe-eau 17; ~ **skiing** le ski nautique 84

way *(finding the ~)* 64; ~ **in** l'entrée 83 f; ~ **out** la sortie 72,83
W.C. les W.C. *mpl* 17,24,64
we nous 7,95
weather le temps 93; ~ **forecast** le bulletin météo 77
week la semaine 9,71,72,92; ~**-end** le weekend
weights 36,39
welcome bienvenu/e
well bien 88; **as** ~ aussi
west l'ouest m 63
wet mouillé/e, humide
what qu'est-ce que; ~ **is it?** qu'est-ce que c'est? 24,88,89,91,bc
wheat le blé
wheel la roue 69; **spare** ~ la roue de secours; ~**-chair** le fauteuil roulant 7
when quand, à quelle heure 13,74,75,79,bc
where où 43,63,64,74,75,88,bc
which quel/quelle 74
who qui; ~ **is it?** qui est-ce? 55,bc
whose à qui
why pourquoi; ~ **not** pourquoi pas bc
wife la femme 87
to **win** gagner
wind le vent 77,93; ~**-surfing** la planche à voile 84
window la fenêtre 16
wine le vin 23,29,89
winter l'hiver m 93; ~ **sports** les sports *mpl* d'hiver 85
with avec 10,56
without sans 35
woman la femme, la dame 64
wonderful merveilleux/-euse 89
wood le bois, la forêt 62
wool la laine
I **work** je travaille *(travailler)*; **to** ~ *(things)* marcher, fonctionner 15,70
to **write** écrire 52,bc; **in writing** par écrit
wrong 28; **you're** ~ vous vous êtes trompé/e

Y

yacht le yacht 76-77,84
year l'an m, l'année f, 80,87; **New** ~ 93
yesterday hier 92
not **yet** pas encore
yogurt le yaourt 42
you vous (tu) 58,90,95; **your** votre (ton/ta) 95
youth hostel l'auberge f de jeunesse 21

Z

zip la fermeture éclair
zoo le zoo

0	zéro *zayro*	18	dix-huit *deez-**weet***	100	cent *song*
1	un, une *uhn, uwn*	19	dix-neuf *deez-**nurf***	101	cent un *song **uhn***
2	deux *dur*	20	vingt *vang*	500	cinq cents *sank song*
3	trois *trwa*	21	vingt et un *vantay-**uhn***	510	cinq cent* dix *sank song **deece***
4	quatre *kattr*	22	vingt-deux *vant **dur***	1000	mille *meel*
5	cinq *sank*	23	vingt-trois *vant **trwa***	1100	mille cent *meel song*
6	six *seece*	30	trente *tront*	1960	mille neuf cent* soixante *meel nurf song swassont*
7	sept *set*	40	quarante *karront*		
8	huit *weet*	50	cinquante *sangkont*	2000	deux mille *dur meel*
9	neuf *nurf*	60	soixante *swassont*	2001	deux mille un *dur meel **uhn***
10	dix *deece*	70	soixante-dix *swassont-**deece***	1 000 000	un million *uhn meel-yong*
11	onze *awnz*	71	soixante et onze *swassont ay **awnz***		*no s
12	douze *dooz*	72	soixante-douze *swassont **dooz***		
13	treize *trez*	80	quatre-vingts *kattr-**vang***		
14	quatorze *kattorz*	81	quatre-vingt-un *kattr vang **tuhn***		
15	quinze *kanz*	82	quatre-vingt-deux *kattr vang **dur***	1st	premier/première *prumyay/prumyair*
16	seize *sez*	90	quatre-vingt-dix *kattr vang **deece***	2nd	deuxième *durz-yem*
17	dix-sept *dee-**set***	91	quatre-vingt-onze *kattr vang **awnz***	3rd	troisième *trwaz-yem*